HAPPY
EVERYTHING

DEBBY CARUSO

D1522819

ISBN-13: 978-1-7325190-2-2
Book cover design and interior formatting by Tugboat Design

For Scott, Enzo, and Dagny
My very own
Holy Trinity

Chapter One

"Are you sure you want to do this?" I reach across the café table and squeeze her hand, holding her gaze as I stir my latte. "I mean, are you sure you want to do it *like* this?"

"I truly believe it's the best option," she nodded. "And you know I never wanted the big to-do anyway. That's you, my friend. That was never really me." She sighed and then smiled big and pretty.

"Yes…I ah, I tend to over-do."

"You?"

"Me."

"Never." She shakes her head vehemently, and then we laughed the laugh of old friends who don't need to embellish.

"Come on, back to work." I grab what was left of my latte and give her a sort-of-side-hug-pat-on-the-shoulder thing as we exit our favorite coffee place.

As we walk back to work, I marvel over the fact that we never seemed to tire of each other; Dez and I work together, we hang out together when we aren't working, and we celebrate almost every holiday together.

Translation: I force Dez to come to my house and be my wingwoman for every holiday I possibly can. Every possible event, made-up holiday or real, I somehow manage to coerce my very best friend into being a part of my chaos.

Friends really are the very best family.

I count myself lucky as we part and go off to finish brainstorming the latest grand scheme: a new way to sell protein bars in an already crowded marketplace. I sigh deeply as I take in my cluttered desk, knowing that I need to get organized in order to put my brain to work.

Thankfully, I am saved by the phone. I dive for it when I see that it's James.

"Hey! I just called you on your cell but it went straight to voice mail. Were you in a meeting?" He says this by way of greeting.

"Well, hello to you too..." I act huffy but I'm sure to be betrayed by the smile in my voice. "I was in the elevator."

"Gotcha. Hey, listen...do you want to meet me for a quick bite after work? I have to meet Jack later–because he's getting out much later–but I thought maybe we can grab something together and then I'll meet you later on back at the house."

"That sounds good. Wait, why are you meeting Jack?"

"Not sure. Look, babe, I've got to go. Love you, see you later." He hangs up and I sigh again.

Okay. Well...I take a deep breath and dive into the first pile of paper that has formed a Mt. Vesuvius on the front left corner of my desk. I don't know why I do this, but I do it all the time: allow myself to stack papers until they resemble some sort of messy design, insist that I can find anything at a moment's notice in said pile, and then eventually dismantle the pile when I realize that the clutter is killing my creative vibe. I start sorting and at the same time my brain begins to think about the protein powerhouse that we need to create a new ad campaign for...what are they looking for again?

Something fresh.

Something new.

Something safe is what they're not saying out loud, because they came across as wanting to play it safe, and yet somehow, we're supposed to create a fresh, new approach to safe and... boring.

This should be fun.

$\mathcal{C}$hapter $\mathcal{T}$wo

The quick-bite go-to place that James and I frequent far too often is a neighborhood bistro with fresh food galore. It helps me to stay on track, unless of course they trot out an amazing new flatbread which I am powerless to resist.

I enter the bistro and see James over by the bar ordering us both a glass of wine. He turns and looks over his shoulder as I make my way towards our favorite table, offering me a wink and a smile. I smile back as I shrug off my coat, place it over my chair, and greet our usual waiter. By the time James joins me with the wine, I have two glasses of water with lemon already on the table.

"Well, hello gorgeous," he greets me as if he hasn't seen me for ages.

This–and this alone–is enough to make me swoon, and in so doing, I remind myself that we've got a pretty good thing going. We've been married almost two years, and I still feel as if we're in the honeymoon phase. Don't get me wrong; that doesn't mean that he knows how to make dishes jump from the sink into the dishwasher. He doesn't. And his mother…well, let's just say that if Vivian is the price I have to pay for the love of this man…most days he's totally worth it.

"So where are you off to after this?" I never really got a chance to talk to him today and details are not his strong suit either way.

"I'm meeting Jack for a drink downtown. He's been working on this project at a school, and they generally do all the noisy stuff after the school is closed, so his hours right now are shifted." He shrugs.

"Yes, Dez told me that he'll be on the job down there for a few more weeks and then it's back to waking up at the crack of dawn." I roll my eyes. The mere idea of getting up that early hurts my face. "I think he wants to talk to you about the wedding."

"Did they decide?" He looks up as he's giving the menu a cursory glance. I don't know why he bothers when we both know we're ordering the flatbread special.

"I think so. She says so." I shrug myself. "I just don't want her to regret anything."

"Look Rhonda," James pauses here, takes a sip of his drink, then dives in. "Not everyone wants the fairytale white wedding with the hundreds of guests and the entire obligation that goes along with it."

"I get that. It's just…" I trail off here, because I know James knows some of Dez's backstory, but I know all of it, and I find myself not wanting to betray her confidence, even to him.

It's a story in some ways typical: Dez's Mom Amalia meets a man, falls in love, he ends up emotionally abusing her, she stays, eventually they break up, they get back together, she realizes he's an alcoholic, then he realizes he's an alcoholic, he has another girlfriend, she finds out, they break up, they get back together, always running back to Amalia...and now he's currently residing in a faraway rehabilitation center. This would all be well and good, as per Dez, but the problem at hand is that he's getting out soon and intending to go back to Amalia a 'changed person.'

Dez doesn't trust him as far as she could throw him (and believe me, she'd like to throw him very, very far) but the bigger issue is actually her mother. Her mother cannot see why Dez is not interested in giving this cretin another chance and therefore this has driven a wedge between them.

Hence the destination wedding that Dez is gunning for: no surprise guests, no surprise fights, nothing that Dez can't control. I get her and I don't blame her; I'm just not so sure Jack is completely onboard.

"I know you love your friend. We all do, and I think Jack just wants to talk to me about the whole thing one more time before they make a final decision." James breaks into a genuine grin. "Of course, I'm pushing him towards St. Lucia."

"Of course you are." I shake my head.

"It'll be a great getaway for us, and you have to admit that we both need a serious vacation." James reaches across the table for my hand at the same moment the waiter delivers the flatbread.

"Ooooh," we both exclaim, then drop hands quickly.

There is no talking for a full minute as we practically inhale the latest incarnation of our midweek fave. I let my mind wander as I chew, thinking about our last big trip, and then I picture a Caribbean beach, the water perfectly blue.

"We definitely need another." I'm talking about a serious vacation.

"Definitely," he agrees and raises his arm in order to get the waiter's attention.

It takes a full minute before I realize that he's talking about the flatbread.

Chapter Three

As I walk past the conference room the next day at work, I see everyone from my team swarming around the long table, heads down, rooting through what looks to be various types of baskets.

I pop my head in. "Hey, what are you guys doing?"

"Perfect Protein sent us some samples," Lola seems overly excited by this, her fists full of little bars in crinkly wrappers.

"I will bet money they all taste like cardboard," Ramon says with utter conviction, and Lola shoots him the daggers. "I only came in here because I thought there might be some leftover birthday cake."

"Ramon, it's eleven in the morning," I point out.

"So? It's basically the same stuff people put in pancakes. It's never too early for cake!" He looks at me as if I have lost my mind.

"I guess." I walk past him and Lola and peer into the newly decimated baskets. I pull out a protein bar labeled raspberry cheesecake. I see a Key Lime pie, but it doesn't really grab my interest the way cheesecake does and probably always will.

I love cheesecake. Period.

I root around for another minute, grabbing Major Mocha for Dez, and then make the trek over to her office. She seems to be the only one working, and I have an idea I want to bounce off her.

"Dez!" I call out to her as I come through the door, waving my protein offering. She gives me the one-sec sign and then makes a few noncommittal noises before hanging up the phone.

"Hey," she says and then shoves a clipboard away from her, pulling a face. "I don't know that I'm making my life any easier by having a destination wedding. What's that?" She points to the mocha bar.

I toss it over to her and she catches it. "It's our new client. Perfect Protein. Have you ever tried their bars?"

"No. What flavor is this, Styrofoam or plywood?" She turns the bar over and begins inspecting the ingredients.

"I bought you mocha." I shoot her a look. "I took a raspberry cheesecake for myself, would you rather try that?"

"I'd rather have an actual piece of real-life raspberry cheesecake."

"It's eleven in the morning," I find myself pointing out again.

"So? Isn't it basically the same stuff they put in pancakes?"

I groan before I answer her. "Listen, Artie's breezing in here about two-ish, and we're supposed to meet for some sort of pow-wow in the conference room about then. Did you read his text?" Artie is our boss, the Big Man on Campus who is given to the dramatic, and acts as if everything is a tragedy. He is also our biggest cheerleader, and we tend to love him in spite of himself.

"Yes. Heavy on the –ish." She gives me a fabulous eye roll.

"Okay, so that being what it is, I'm going to go work on some ideas while I taste-test a bar or two. Are you in?"

"I can be in if we grab a cappuccino to wash down the bar." She's already grabbing her purse, knowing my answer to caffeine is always a firm yes.

We trot downstairs and order the usual, then rip apart the shiny little packages that are supposed to represent a treat.

We watch each other intently as we chew, and chew, and chew.

"Chewy," she says, her mouth still full.

"Definitely chewy," I nod in agreement.

We simultaneously take a deep sip of our coffee. Then we take another bite and chew for what seems like forever.

"Your thoughts?" I indicate the wrapper that she is currently balling up in her fist.

"Look, if I had to choose between that and any other form of real food, the real food would win," she sighs. "But they're not awful. Once again, we're just going to have to do our magic."

"I feel like everything that needs to be said about protein bars has already been said." I take my wrapper and shoot it into the nearby receptacle. "Five points!"

Chapter Four

We're about to exit the coffee shop when I pick up my phone to see that Uncle Ben has sent me another meme about wine. I'm texting him back as we're grabbing our stuff, so I don't even see my father until I almost bang into him.

"Dad!" I exclaim. "Hey there! Sorry, I almost nailed you. What are you doing here?" For some reason, I thought he was out of town.

"Oh, hey...Miss Golden," he leans in to give me a quick kiss-hug combination but the whole thing is off for some reason. His voice, his hug...hell, even a quick glance at his tie makes my antennae go up.

He doesn't answer me but does this strange sort of dance in place, his eyes darting everywhere except to look in my face.

"Do you have a minute? Want to join us?" I indicate Dez, still sipping her coffee as she's gathering her stuff. She offers him a quick wave. In the second it takes me to turn back to my father, there is quite suddenly a woman standing by his side.

"I, ah…" He seems flushed. "Rhonda, this is my friend Julia. Julia, this is Rhonda."

"Oh, hey there. Nice to meet you," I offer my hand. She shakes it vigorously and flashes a big smile full of blindingly white teeth.

"Nice to meet you!" she responds, somewhere between overly friendly and gushing.

"And we've got to get going!" my father pronounces as if he's a game show host going to commercial.

I nod my head and take him in again, quickly, stare at her for a couple of beats, then remember my manners and say, "Well, I'll give you a buzz later."

"Yes! Later is good!" He practically shoves her out the door in front of him and in an instant they are gone.

I turn around to find Dez standing right beside me, still holding onto her cappuccino while giving him the side-eye.

"What the hell was that?" She nods towards him, a confused expression on her face.

"I'm not really sure." I try to shrug it off, but I know my father pretty well, and something was definitely up.

Chapter Five

"So what was your week like?" James asks as he balances his coffee on his chest.

We're doing our favorite Saturday morning thing: backed into opposite ends of the couch, we've got our legs piled on top of each other, nuzzling feet and blankets. The television is on but muted, and I've just managed to make a spectacular round of coffee and settle myself back into our little couch nest.

"Hectic. The usual. Artie picked up the Perfect Protein account, and that's the next thing on my plate," I shrug. "No pun intended."

"How long have we been married?" James raises his eyebrows. "There's always a pun intended."

I chuck a pillow at his head and it sails over the couch.

"You're lucky; I didn't want to spill your coffee."

He makes a noise and then shifts to carefully place his coffee on the table made for it. I take note of the coaster usage and realize he's hoping for a mid-morning ah...cuddle.

We begin to kiss and then he slowly takes my coffee out of my hand and joins it next to his. I smile and then invite him under my blanket. Just as I'm about to suggest moving the party elsewhere, the home phone rings.

"I thought we were getting rid of the home phone," I murmur. Although there's a way to turn off the ringer on the landline, I always forget to do it, and the ring seems shrill and ostentatious in comparison to the current ringtone on my cell.

"We are. We will." He's trying to ignore it, I can tell.

"Grab it if you need to," I say. I pull away but still feel his warmth on top of me.

"Stay. Right. There." He instructs me as he heaves himself off the couch and lunges for the nearest handset. "Hello?"

I think briefly about getting up and jumping back into bed–meeting him there instead–but I notice the shift in his tone immediately and know for sure that I don't need to ask who's on the line.

Vivian.

Vivian is my mother-in-law, my sometime nemesis, and either way, the woman with the worst timing in the entire universe.

"Since when do we have Family Meetings?" I hear James asking her in a tone that he reserves only for her.

I burrow myself down into the blankets and sigh. Talk about a buzzkill. I reach out for my coffee again and take a long sip.

"Okay, well…no, I don't think. Can you hold on a second while I check?" He cradles the phone to his chest and turns to me. "Do we have any plans for tonight?"

"Nothing we can't change," I shrug. We were going to meet Dez and Jack and her cousins from out of town for tapas, but worst-case scenario they could always go without us.

I sit up, blatantly eavesdropping now, wondering what's going on with Vivian, but he's turned his back to me and is currently making noises into the phone, with no actual words.

A moment later he hangs up the phone and gives me a confused look as he slumps back down onto the couch.

"In case you haven't figured that out yet, my mother just called a 'Family Meeting' for tonight," he sighs as he grabs his coffee and lifts himself back off the couch in search of a quick reheat from the microwave.

"I've never heard her call for a 'Family Meeting' before." I wrap it in quotes like he did.

"Perhaps because there's no such thing?" He opens his arms wide, then turns and lifts the coffee out of the microwave. "I swear she's gotten more dramatic as she ages. Most people give up drama as they get older. But not my mother; she actually seems as if she's diving into the deep end of the drama pool."

"Well, we'll pacify her then." I'm already texting Dez, knowing she can go out with her cousin Valentina and her latest beau (Omar the Magician) without us and still have a relatively decent time.

I mean, it won't be the same, but...I allow myself a chuckle as I add a GIF that I think is funny. Dez gets this whole thing with Vivian, and she knows that there will always be a story to tell after the fact. So at least there's a tiny payoff...because with Vivian...there's always a story.

Chapter Six

"What are you making?" James walks into the kitchen and sniffs.

"Some good old-fashioned Candy Shop Brownies," I reply, knowing full well that I've made his day with that one sentence.

"Yes!" He pumps his fist in the air as if his team won the championship. "Are they done yet?"

"No," I shoo him away. "Go get in the shower." I swat his behind as he passes me. I continue cleaning up but my mind begins to wander, and I wonder what exactly we're in for tonight. After making apologies to Dez, I texted Uncle Ben, and he said that he'd see me over there too. Could Vivian and Vlad be getting divorced? I mull that over for a few minutes but then dismiss it because although Vivian is insufferable more often than not, Vlad seems to be the only person who actually knows how to deal with her.

Maybe they're moving! Oh, I forgot about that big push to move to Florida that they both went through about a year back: Vivian's friend Marjorie and her husband Mack had moved down to Florida last year, and once Vivian and Vlad had gone to visit, they both became rather interested in the South Florida real estate market. Unfortunately, that lasted about six weeks, and then hurricane season hit, in which case Vivian decided she would rather deal with northern winters.

I load the dishwasher and wipe down the cabinets. I knew I was wasting my time ruminating; with Vivian it could range from totally earth-shattering to something that wouldn't even bother most people. James was right when he said that she was given to drama, and lately, it seemed as if she had ratcheted up her game a bit.

I shrug as the timer goes off on the brownies. Either way, I was sure to find out soon enough. I pull the brownies from the oven and insert a butter knife directly into the center of the pan. When it comes out clean, I smile, thinking of how my mother had taught me all the little things, and how I was grateful to her in everything. The Candy Shoppe Brownies were her own concoction: one year, we had so much Halloween candy left over, she decided to make use of it by chopping various snack-sized bars into little bits of Heaven, then lacing them throughout a brownie mix, as well as sprinkling some on top. They were a huge hit for some event my mother was a part of, and they soon became my father's favorite, as I began to make them for him every year around his birthday. I knew they'd go over well at Vivian's; she was not one to dabble in the realm of homemade food, but had a real sweet tooth that she liked to indulge every minute she could. Since marrying James, I had become quite good at predicting what platters she would order from her friendly neighborhood deli–that was her go-to meal whenever we went over there–but for some reason she never ordered dessert, so I took that as my cue to bring something over whenever we were summoned.

Chapter Seven

By the time we cut through traffic and are further delayed at an accident scene, we're the last to arrive at Vivian and Vlad's, and James is starting to get antsy, which I knew from experience led straight to hangry. My biggest issue upon arrival is desperately needing to pee, so once we get through the door and say hello, I escape the double-kiss vortex and power-walk as fast as I can to the powder room. Moments later, I exit to find Vivian holding court in her front living area, my husband already shoving a hastily thrown together sandwich down his throat. James gestures to the space on the sofa next to him, and as I cross the room, I'm surprised to see Ira and Jill assembled on a nearby loveseat.

"Oh, hey! I didn't know you guys were–" I was about to give them each a quick hug, but was summarily cut off by Vivian.

"Rhonda, not now." Vivian always looked as if she was sucking lemons, but her current state of face was one for the record books. She points to the seat next to James. She shakes her head, clears her throat, and continues.

"As all of you know, I've asked you to this Family Meeting because we have an issue that must be dealt with, a tragedy of sorts..." another face, this one I couldn't interpret, then, as only Vivian could: "Aunt Bunny has cancer."

There was a moment when I believe the entire world stopped turning and utter silence filled the room. For once, Vivian didn't seem as if she were auditioning for a role as an aging soap opera actress. Then everyone begins speaking at once. In the next few minutes we find out that Aunt Bunny has a very treatable form of breast cancer that they had caught early, and is scheduled for surgery in the coming weeks, with more decisions to be made after that.

"Uncle Ben, how are you holding up?" James crosses the room to envelop his Uncle in a long-held bear hug.

"I'm okay," He pats James on the back and then steps away from him, looking him square in the eye. "We're going to be okay."

From then on, there are hugs all around, and eventually we all dig into the various platters Vivian had ordered. By the time we put out the Candy Shoppe Brownies, Vivian is three Toasted Almonds in and Uncle Ben and James were about to finish off a bottle of red. I'm nursing a glass of white wine in a big comfy chair and taking in each member of the family as they sit and talk, joke and console. I find myself ruminating on all sorts of things, but what keeps coming to mind is this: these are the people who populate my life. For better or worse, they're my family now, and I am a part of this tribe. I toast all of them, silently, knowing that there would be many days ahead when we would need to lean on each other, and I find that I am strangely okay with it.

Chapter Eight

"So how are you holding up?" I'm driving back from Vivian's as I didn't drink nearly as much as James, not that I could blame him.

"I'm okay," he spoke with a sigh in his voice. "I'm sorry that it happened to her."

"Me too," I take my right hand off the steering wheel for a moment and pat his knee. "But the good news is that it seems like they caught it early."

"Sure," he agrees but I could tell he was fading at this point and not really paying too much attention to the words coming out of my mouth. We were home before we knew it, as there was no traffic and the accident we encountered on the way there had completely cleared up. Once I parked we made our way inside and got ready for bed in a tired kind of quiet, each of us lost in our own thoughts.

I woke up to Uncle Ben texting me thanks for the brownies:

Your brownies paired perfectly with the Syrah. Perhaps a bit too perfect.

I laugh and smile. I text him back a picture of a bottle of Advil.

He sends me back a laugh emoticon.

Over coffee, James and I speak about all sorts of things, from Aunt Bunny's treatment, to the guy that we needed to come and fix the microwave door...work, Dez and Jack's wedding... and eventually we circled around to being there for Uncle Ben. We linger and cuddle and sigh a lot. Although James had lost his grandfather mere months after we got married, we hadn't had to deal with a serious family situation yet. You could argue that there was always something going on as far as Vivian was concerned, but real or contrived, we both knew that what Aunt Bunny was going through was no comparison to Vivian-level heartache.

We order Chinese takeout sometime early evening, and eventually settle in for some Sunday night television. We didn't talk much, but as I rested my head on his chest, I heard his heart beat like a drum, and I felt that maybe it would all turn out okay.

Chapter Nine

"I need a mop and bucket in Aisle Ten! STAT!" I shout into the intercom first thing Monday morning, trying to summon Dez with my effervescent charm.

"I don't speak to anybody who confuses supermarket urgency with a true medical emergency," Dez states loud and clear, "...at least not until I have a cup of coffee."

"I can fix that!" I hit the release button and grab my purse, practically trotting over to Dez's office.

"Oh Dear God," Dez groans when I throw open her door. "Whatever has gotten into you? Not to sound like a jackass, but I would have thought you'd be a bit more morose this morning."

"Do you want me to be depressed? I'm concerned, sure, but I have an idea. And it's making me feel better. So-"

"Oh no you don't."

"You don't even know what my idea is yet!"

"It doesn't matter. If it involves me in any way...the answer is *no*."

"Let me buy you a coffee."

"Won't work."

"Should I sweeten the deal?"

"I have my own coffee app, thanks. In fact, I think I get a free scone tomorrow."

"But Dez! Hear me out at least!"

"I will. Caffeine first, then you get your audience with the Queen."

"Fair enough."

I let her take a nice long sip and even give her a moment to let the caffeine work its way through her veins before I dive in again.

"Did you know that the first night of Passover falls on Good Friday this year?" I drop the bomb and then sit back and wait for her reaction.

Dez never disappoints.

"Do. Not. Even. Think. IT!" she practically shouts at me, each word punctuated by a bounce up and down in her favorite cozy chair that she frequents.

"But—"

"There will be NO BUTS!" she's practically snarling at me. "Have you learned absolutely nothing by the last holiday debacle?"

"That's my point exactly," I try to usher in my most reassuring tone. "I learned so much! I am now the proud host of The Most Fabulous Last Night of Hanukkah on the planet," I say, beaming with pride.

"Then let's leave it at that and call it a win," Dez suggests in a tone that is slightly more civil.

"Well…I can't now. Aunt Bunny and Uncle Ben always host

Passover, and we all know that this year she just won't be up to it, so…" I trail off, hands in the air.

"Then let Vivian order platters from the kosher deli," Dez suggests this as if it's a real suggestion.

"We can't have deli on Passover!"

"Why not? We have pizza on Hanukkah!"

"Dez," I take a deep breath and sigh, "You know it's the right thing to do."

"For who?"

"For everyone. For Aunt Bunny and Uncle Ben. For James and I. For all of us!" I exclaim loud enough that the woman sitting next us no longer has her head buried in her laptop, but is currently tossing me a significant glare.

"I notice you didn't mention Vivian and Vlad," Dez grimaces in a way that I can't help but laugh at; she's right, and we both know it.

"Them too," I concede, but I'm giggling now, knowing I should feel some sense of shame.

"Uh-huh. Tell that to someone who doesn't know you very well." With that, Dez takes a final swig of her coffee and then shows me all her teeth. "I'm actually getting a refill before we head back to the shark-infested waters upstairs. Considering how my day began, I need to be ready for all of it."

"You act as if I'm a raving lunatic!" I protest, once again, a bit too loud for Laptop Lady, considering the intensified glare.

"And if the sneaker fits…" she's striding to the counter now, her back to me, but I know she loves me in spite of…well…me.

Chapter Ten

"Honey!" I greet James with a glass of wine in my hand, which just happens to be one of his favorites.

"Sweetie!" He counters, giving me a quick kiss on the cheek while extricating the wine. "It's been a helluva Monday…how'd you know?"

I know nothing, but it's never a bad idea to approach James with a glass of his current favorite and a smile on my face. I kept thinking about waiting until the weekend to pitch my plan, but I knew I wouldn't be able to hold it in all week long, so I settled instead for some subliminal bribery.

"And I made you a weeknight favorite…" I trail off as I head into the kitchen, checking the oven, then getting ready to plate.

"To what do I owe the pleasure…?" He is squinting at me now, and I simply continue to smile as I heap his plate full of both ooey and gooey.

"It's a Monday. You know? Mondays are generally sucky. So I decided to make this one less so," I shrug as if that's all I have up my three-quarter-sleeve.

"Rhonda, my love," James pulls me into an embrace, as I try to make sure my spatula doesn't hit him in the back of his neck. "I know you so much better than that. What gives?"

"Well, let's go sit down," I break free, grab my wine and plate, and tilt my head for him to follow. He follows me to our tiny kitchen table, placing his wine and plate down, and then hurries back to grab two napkins and forks. I wait for him to take a big bite before I begin my pitch.

"So! You know how we were talking about finding ways to support Aunt Bunny and Uncle Ben? I had a tremendous idea this morning and I couldn't wait to share it with you!" I am good at building excitement in the board room and hope that it carries over here.

He's nodding and chewing, which I take as a cue to go on.

"I think we should offer to host Passover here!" I deliver this on the quick, not giving him a second to interrupt. "I looked at the calendar this morning and I realized that this year Passover begins the same night as Good Friday! So we can have everyone here for dinner on Friday and then still host brunch on Easter Sunday. What do you think?" I feel myself getting excited as visions of recipes begin dancing through my head.

"I think I don't want to overstep," he sighs. "I honestly don't know what the right thing to do is here," James takes a sip of his wine and I fall silent, thinking it through.

"Are you saying that you think that Aunt Bunny would feel like I was trying to take Passover away from her?" I hadn't even thought of anything remotely like that.

"I mean, I guess because nobody knows anything yet, I don't

want to suppose. I don't want her to feel as if we're treating her like she can't do it, because she's sick...and I'm not sure what to do," he offers me a tiny smile. "I wish there was an etiquette site online for what to do for people who have cancer."

"There probably is one," I muse. "Either way, I totally get it." My enthusiasm just took a nose dive, but I have to agree, and I'm not willing to make Aunt Bunny feel any worse than she already does.

"How about this?" James suggests. "I'll talk to Uncle Ben and see if they have a date for her surgery yet, and then we'll go from there. In the meantime, do you want to start planning Easter brunch?"

"Sure!" I polish off my last few bites. When I place my fork down, I look him deep in the eyes and say, "James, you know I only want to help, right?"

"I know your heart's in the right place," he leans over his dish and plants a kiss somewhere between cheek and nose. "Now how about another glass?"

I hold up my wine glass for him to fill. All in all, not a totally sucky Monday.

Chapter Eleven

By the time I'm ready to create a cohesive sentence, I get interrupted by Ramon banging on my door, or rather trying to ram the door open with a huge box in his arms.

"What the...?" I jump up to try and help as he practically drops the box at my feet.

"Perfect Protein just sent a boatload of new flavors, and I've been assigned the job of taking them all and distributing them around the office. You're my first stop," Ramon says as he begins to open the flaps. "Have at it."

I dive in and begin to peruse all the flavors I haven't seen before: Monkey Madness, The Kitchen Sink, and Bodacious Brownie end up on my desk, but then I take a second glance and see one called The Go-Go.

"The Go-Go?" I look to Ramon but he only offers me a noncommittal shrug. "Have you actually tried any of these?"

"I'm avoiding them like the plague," he offers in typical Ramon fashion.

"Okay, but how are we going to sell them then?" I counter.

"Did we eat the pillows when we did that whole Pillow Talk campaign?"

"Ah, no, but…"

"Exactly." With that, he heaves the box off the floor and continues to make his rounds. By the time he makes it over to Dez, she buzzes me and suggests lunch, which I agree to in a flash. I still need to tell her what James said about the upcoming holidays.

We rush out to street level and quickly get on line at our favorite salad spot. Once we point, pick, and wait for our custom-made salads, we settle into the first two chairs we can find. Neither one of us says a word as we tear into the salads as if we haven't eaten in years.

"I am so hungry," Dez offers between bites. "What is it about work? It's as if sitting at my desk for more than twenty minutes leads me into the land of famine, and just when I think it'll never happen again, there's tomorrow." She stuffs a few more forkfuls in her mouth.

"Did you try any of the new bars yet?" I say between bites myself.

"No, I haven't had time," she stops long enough to down some water. "You?"

"Not yet," I reply. "Ramon seems like a big fan though."

At that, we both stop to laugh. Ramon is our office curmudgeon, and although he drives us all nuts most of the time, he also happens to be brilliant, which is why Artie keeps him.

"I'm going to try one later on with coffee," Dez announces.

"I'll do the same." I polish off the last few bites and then decide to share. "So: I broached the subject of Passover with James last night and—"

"He's having you committed next week?" she offers, as if it's a strong possibility.

"Ha! You're a riot," I ball up a napkin and manage to hit her on the nose. "Five points. Anyway, he said something I hadn't even thought of...that he didn't want to make Aunt Bunny feel bad, or incapacitated, or sicker than she already was..."

"Valid point."

"True. So he said he's going to ask Uncle Ben and then we'll go from there," I shrug. "We agreed to start planning Easter brunch though."

"Sounds like a plan," Dez indicates the time and we get up to leave.

"Are you guys going to come over for Brunch?"

"I'm not sure yet. You know Jack's originally from Maine, right? He mentioned wanting to go up there but from what I gather it'll still be cold at Easter, so...we'll see. Plus his family makes me nervous. They're so...functional."

I stifle a smile. That was the best I was going to get from Dez, so I let it lie for the time being. We have a meeting in about an hour with Artie and Team Perfect Protein, so we shuffle back to work quickly and then make a plan to meet up right before the meeting so we can grab a coffee and split a bar.

When I get back to my office there's a voicemail from my father and a pile of mail on my desk. I try my father back, and when he doesn't pick up I leave him a voicemail in return. I remind myself to invite him over for Easter. It's still a few weeks away, but I know my father forgets things like holidays that aren't the same date every year, so I'll be sure to bug him. The next thing I know, Dez is buzzing me, and I grab a Go-Go bar from the pile and do just that.

Chapter Twelve

"We have a situation," Artie announces by way of greeting, only his tone sounds as if we are all currently locked in a submarine and about to perish.

All eyes are already on him, but he takes a moment to review the troops one by one before speaking again. Artie was once a sought-after theatre actor, then swung into voice-overs in order to pay the bills, and from there met a whole slew of people in the advertising industry. One thing led to another, and although Artie eventually became a legend in advertising...most days I think Artie still thinks he's on stage.

He waits a beat more and then proceeds, "Perfect Protein wants us to do a flavor contest." He makes a face that indicates just how odious he finds this idea.

"Like M&M's?" Lola asks as she almost vaults off her chair with what could only be characterized as glee.

"What are you talking about?" Ramon can barely hide his disgust in general, but her sudden excitement almost puts him out indefinitely.

"How do you not know about this?" She's horrified but not speechless. "Every year the M&M brand launches three new flavors and asks the public to try them and vote on them. Generally, the one that does the best in the trial gets turned into a permanent flavor," she continues, "and so far I've predicted all the ones that won!"

It's like she won the Oscar. I've actually never seen Lola get so excited about anything.

"Although that's a fabulous asset," Artie presses on as though Lola's sheer glee hasn't even registered, "how about we focus our energy on *this* brand? Look, you all know how I hate contests and things of this sort...they're so...gimmicky, for lack of a better word...and the truth is that nobody ever wins. What do you win? A flavor they already made? The feeling of being a 'winner?'" he blanches in time with the air quotes.

I can't even look at Lola, so I try to focus on our cheerless leader.

"Either way, here's what I need all of you to begin working on: Perfect Protein wants a campaign based around this whole idea of their taste, and then of course, we need to mention the convenience factor. I still haven't hammered out specifics, but this little brouhaha should in effect get your engines running. Okay? Okay!" With that, he strides from the room, leaving the rest of us still seated and staring after him.

"I hate protein bars," Alex says as he gets up and saunters after Artie. Alex is yet another brilliant artist on our team that doesn't say a whole lot, but can put together a storyboard like no one I know.

"Don't we all?" Ramon follows suit.

I look at Dez and shrug, "I think I've got to try a few more before I make a decision."

"It's like dating," Lola casually puts in. "You need to try a bunch of flavors before you find the one you really like."

Indeed.

Chapter Thirteen

For some strange reason, the box bearing a myriad of protein bars wound its way back to my office, so I decide to grab a couple of handfuls before I leave for the day and throw them in a bag, figuring I will pawn some off on James and see what he thinks.

In other words: a little market research.

By the time I arrive home, James is already there unloading some takeout Thai and I couldn't be more pleased. It's a Tuesday, and I feel as if this week will last forever.

"Thanks, babe," I say as it's my turn to grab the napkins and forks. "I think I needed this. How'd you know?"

"Well, I didn't know, but I'm glad I did," he says as we transfer food to plate. "Listen, I spoke to Uncle Ben at lunch, and he said that Aunt Bunny's surgery is scheduled for next Thursday."

"Okay. Should we take off work?" I'm already shuffling through my mind for all the things that I may need to take care of in order to take the day.

"No," he chews, grabs a sip, then finishes, "I'm going to hang out with him while she's in, then I think we should invite him over for dinner that night. Do you think you could take care of dinner?"

"Sure. Are you sure you don't want me to come along?" I'm pretty sure I'm a good hand-holder.

"You really don't need to be there," he shakes his head as he continues, "and you should thank me for sparing you. My Mom and Vlad will be there all day, and I wouldn't want to subject you to that."

We laugh, and I feel bad for a quick second but then I realize that he knows who they are, and he actually is sparing me.

"Should I plan on them for dinner as well?" I can make enough food to feed an army if that's what the day calls for.

"I'm thinking no..." he hesitates. "Well, let me get back to you on that. I mean, I'd much rather it just be us and Uncle Ben. I figured I'd uncork some red and drive him home right before he starts to nod off. I figure it'll be a long day."

"My understanding with a lumpectomy is that she'll only spend one night in the hospital," I put in.

"If that. Uncle Ben said that the surgery itself only takes an hour, so I'm thinking if they send her home that same day, maybe...can you make something that we can bring over there instead?"

"Absolutely." I'm already thinking lasagna, or perhaps stuffed shells.

"And then Uncle Ben said they might want to do radiation, but we'll cross that bridge when we come to it," James puts down his fork and sighs.

"I know, babe," I put down my fork too and get up from where

I'm sitting to offer him a big hug. He accepts and we stay like that for a while, long enough for me to have to reheat my food. This is foreign territory for both of us; my mother died suddenly, and even though James' grandfather died unexpectedly, he was an old man who had lived a full life. I think it goes without saying that navigating an illness like cancer is an all-new experience for each of us, and we're both heavy with expectation.

"Do you want to hear some good news?" I ask after reheating my plate.

He nods, "Absolutely."

"We're rescheduling Saturday night with Dez and Jack, and this time we're going bowling!"

James groans. I am the one enamored with bowling, while he simply protests vociferously, and in the end still manages to win every time.

"Please tell me that I get to pick the restaurant, at least..." He whines.

"Of course." It's a consolation prize and we both know it, but I offer him a genuine smile, and he laughs at me.

"You're lucky I love you," he shakes his head.

"I am," I say without guile. I'm a very lucky lady, and I know that too.

Chapter Fourteen

The rest of the week flies by, and the next thing I know, we're out with Dez and Jack for Take Two of Tapas.

"We have an announcement to make," Dez and Jack share an intimate look, and then she turns to us and says, "We've decided on St. Lucia."

"Yes!" James practically shouts and then hi-fives Jack, "I propose a toast!"

We all raise our sangria glasses and toast Dez and Jack and their upcoming nuptials.

"When?" I ask, my mind already moving at triple speed, trying to figure out when we'll have her bridal shower.

"May," Dez responds and Jack nods. "We're thinking it'll be perfect timing for everyone, and the weather should be fabulous."

"I'm so excited!" I'm beginning to see it all come together; the bride, the beach, a glorious vacation.

"I'm getting there," Dez finishes her drink and Jack refills her glass in a deft move that I can't help but notice. I love this guy for her, and I'm so happy that he's going to be around forever.

"I can't help feeling a little overwhelmed with the amount of stuff I have to do," she continues, "and I'm a detail girl."

"Exactly! This is precisely why you shouldn't worry. Plus, you've got me! What more can you ask for?" I'm used to juggling all sorts of stuff. I can totally handle helping out Dez.

"Well, I would like to ask you to be my Maid of Honor," Dez has a smile as wide as her face.

I practically lunge across the table to hug her.

"Of course!" It is only fitting; she was mine, and we are basically sisters that were separated at birth.

We hug and kiss and both act as if we're not getting choked up and crying. In the midst of this moment, I see James and Jack hugging and clapping each other on the back, pretending to shed fake tears, and making all sorts of strange noises, all of it ending in a loud round of laughter.

"You guys are idiots," Dez proclaims this but we all laugh, and then Jack announces that James will stand up for him as well.

I come around the table to give Jack a big hug, then hold him at arm's length and look him in the eye, "You mess with her, and I'll kill you with my bare hands." I've said some variation of this several times since they got engaged, and although I'm partially joking, he knows I would find a way if I had to.

"I know this about you, Rhonda. One of the many reasons I adore you," he nods his head, and crushes me in a hug. When we part, we all start discussing the details.

From there, we head to one of my favorite places, which offers bowling with a side of cool. For a guy who professes to hate the sport, James holds his own and manages to beat my score twice.

"We should go," I indicate the time as the guys are trying to decide on another game, "I want to go to church tomorrow."

"Gotcha," James finishes his drink and then we say goodbye to our dearest friends. By the time we get in the car, we're both talking about our nice, comfy bed and warm pillows.

"Is this what it's like to be in our 30's? Or married?" I inquire out loud, not expecting James to answer.

"I think it's both," he smiles at me as he drives. "And I have to tell you I don't mind it one bit. I had fun tonight, but I no longer need to stay out until three in the morning to prove a point."

"I get you. It's just that...when did we ever stay out until three in the morning? I can't remember the last time we did that... maybe on our honeymoon?" I'm shuffling through several scenes in my head, and my mind pauses to remember the third night of our honeymoon. We went from dinner to drinks outside by the pool at our fabulous resort, lingering by a fire pit until another couple we had met earlier came up to us and invited us to the night club. I can clearly remember dancing all night and then ending up at the resort's 24-hour dessert shop and eating crepes sometime around three in the morning.

"Yes. Those crepes were to die for," James makes a longing sound.

"Maybe that should be our goal," I announce with vive. "When we head to St. Lucia, we need to stay up ridiculously late at least one night, and eat something decadent right before we go to bed."

"You got it." With that having been decided, James parks his car and we head inside, eager for the warm bed and fluffy pillows.

Chapter Fifteen

I'm just about to start putting on a dash of makeup when I hear James come up behind me, shuffling sleepily into the bathroom.

"Did I wake you? I'm sorry!" I thought I was using my stealth-getting-ready-skills this morning.

"No," he shakes his head and gives me a hug, his whole body still warm from our piles of blankets, "I've decided to come with you."

"Oh, you don't have to," I protest lightly. I secretly love when James decides to come to church with me but I never ask; I feel I want to respect his religion just as much as he respects mine.

"But I want to," he offers me a quick squeeze and then, "How much time do we have?"

"Fifteen minutes?" I check the clock on my phone.

"I'm in!" He shouts this as he moves quickly from the toilet to the shower, and I chuckle. In the next fifteen minutes, we manage to get ready, leave the house, and somehow there is even a cup of coffee in my hand when we get in the car.

"I say we go to brunch after," I suggest, knowing we will both be hangry by the time we leave the service. Who are these people that don't eat breakfast? I can't imagine being one of them, or being friends with them.

"You got it," James says, "I just wish I had something to tide me over."

"We do!" I suddenly remember the Perfect Protein bars I had thrown in the bag before leaving work the other day. I'm driving this time, so I say to him, "Reach in the backseat and grab that bag. There's a slew of flavors in there; grab one and tell me what you think."

"You're the best!" James exclaims as I hear rustling behind me.

"You haven't tried them yet," I warn.

"Why? Are they gross?" The wrappers crinkle as he shuffles through the pile looking for what grabs him.

"No, not at all. I actually need some feedback. So let me know what you think…honestly."

"Have I ever not been honest?" he quips as he rips open a bar and chews for what seems like forever. He's making noises but no words yet.

"And?" I'm about to park and can't stand the suspense.

"This one is good," he shrugs and shows me the wrapper. The one he chose is Monkey Madness. "Kind of a banana-peanut-butter vibe."

"No cardboard?"

"Nope."

"Good."

He takes a long sip of coffee, reholsters it, and we make our way into church. The church I frequent is in an old building, but the congregation is pretty young, and the music is contemporary and fun.

We find seats and are welcomed by a few people we know, and then I sort of tune into the music and tune out the world. A few songs in, I sneak a look at James and see that he is doing just fine right next to me. My heart swells; I know that this is so unlike any sort of religious experience that James had growing up, and I find myself grateful once again for the man God gave me.

When they offer a prayer line, I whisper to James that I want to go up and have a special prayer of healing said for Aunt Bunny. James accompanies me to the altar, and we bow our heads as the Pastor sends healing, peace, and love energy towards her. As we turn to reclaim our seats, I feel James squeeze my hand. I squeeze back, setting my mind on the positive outcome that we all want: Aunt Bunny rid of cancer, and living a long and healthy life with Uncle Ben.

Chapter Sixteen

After brunch, we head home to a typical Sunday afternoon: leisure time as a couple, a few loads of laundry, a hot cup of tea, and soft piano music playing in the background. It's a lazy afternoon filled with sweet silence, until Vivian shatters it by one of her perfectly timed calls.

"I tried you earlier, where were you?" I can hear Vivian on our end, even though James is holding the phone up to his ear.

"Hmmm…I didn't receive a message," James briefly pulls the phone away from his ear to check the screen.

"Well, I tried your home phone, and no one picked up. Then I got distracted and didn't think to try your cell phone until now. Are you home now? Where were you before?" Her volume is always on high.

"Oh, we were at church and then we went to brunch," James is filling her in absentmindedly as her screech resonates through the line as if she were standing right next to us.

"Church! What do you mean, you went to *church*? Is this

something new?" she huffs and she puffs and I couldn't help but bristle.

"New? No, Mother...I sometimes accompany Rhonda to church the same way she will sometimes go to shul with me. I'm sorry, I didn't catch the reason you called?" James was an expert at handling her, so I allow him to do just that and decide to fold the latest load of laundry to come out of the dryer. I take the laundry basket and dump it on the bed, but find myself fuming as I make solo socks into pairs.

How dare she! Vivian was known to cross the line with me– and let's face it, she has no boundaries with basically anyone– but I really didn't like hearing her admonish James for attending church with me. It was absolutely none of her business how James and I chose to deal with our differences, and either way, how would she feel if she knew that the whole reason I wanted to go to church this morning was to pray for her sister?

I thought about it a moment, then knew that she wouldn't feel the least bit of shame for her outburst no matter what the circumstances. She was one of those truly insufferable people with no filter, and I had to keep reminding myself that she wasn't going to change.

I thought about the famous quote from Gandhi: *Be the change that you wish to see in the world.* And I wanted to laugh, because you really can't be the bigger person while still wishing to throttle someone.

I smooth out one last shirt as James wanders back into our bedroom, and I'm about to speak, but he beats me to it.

"I have no idea what just got into her, but she's in rare form today," he blows out a breath and looks to me for sympathy.

I wasn't sure whether to mention that I heard her outburst or not, but something told me he knew that I heard her, and to simply let it go. I decided to try a different tack.

"Well, maybe she's concerned about Aunt Bunny and she doesn't know how to express herself," I offered, and then realized once I said it that there could be some truth to it.

"She's just too much," James shakes his head and wrings his hands. "I honestly have no idea how Vlad puts up with her."

"Maybe he's the Yin to her Yang," I offer, full of spiritual anecdotes today.

"Maybe," he begins pulling his clothes from the pile and putting them away in his drawers.

"Did she say what she called for...?"

"Yes, at the very end of our conversation she wanted to let me know that David would be in town next Saturday and that she would like us to stop by...apparently, David has a new girlfriend."

"Is she a police officer?" I could hardly see David ending up with anyone else; he was a man who embodied all things law enforcement, in triplicate. James and David were cousins, but they couldn't be more different, and although he enjoyed David's company, it was hard to see anyone enjoying David's company full-time, unless of course they shared the same passion.

"She's an ASPCA cop. At least, I think that's what my mother said. Either way, the point is that they both have off next Saturday, so they're coming to town, and my mother has summoned us."

"All of us?"

"I guess."

"Okay," I plop down on the bed and he closes a drawer, then comes to join me.

"I keep thinking about the whole staying up dancing and eating food that's bad for us but completely delicious at three in the morning," he sighs, "and I wish we had more of it. I feel like we got married, started hosting holidays, paying a mortgage, going to work...we became adults overnight...in a different kind of way, and I'm not so sure I want all of it. Am I making any sense here?"

"Yes, but it's just...Life. The good, the bad, the bills...the family obligations...I think we have to shuffle through the days in order to get to the moments," I sigh too.

"I am looking forward to Dez and Jack's wedding. Really looking forward to it...maybe we can extend our stay," James suggests this as he pulls me in close, and kisses my forehead.

"That might be just what the Doctor ordered," I agree, "Sunshine and indulgence."

"Amen to that."

Chapter Seventeen

"I need all your people," I insist to Dez when we finally have a moment to talk. This week has been crazy, with all of us pushing hard to get a flavor contest off the ground for Perfect Protein, as well as service our other accounts.

"What people? I'm the only Latina I know with three cousins," she laughs as we grab our coffees and make our way over to 'our' spots.

"Ha! Okay, well...I still need phone numbers and whatnot. I'm sure Jack has people, no?" I intend to throw her a great bridal shower, no matter the size.

"I guess," she hesitates, "I feel guilty."

"How?" I'm not following.

"Well, I feel like since I'm not going for the big wedding that I've got some hell of a nerve having a traditional bridal shower." she shrugs. "I'm probably just being weird. All I want is to be with Jack, to have a wedding on the beach, to have the people I love the most surrounding us...I'm pretty unsure about all the rest."

"You can be unsure," I assure her, "because you have me, and I know what you want, and I'm ready and willing to give it to you. You just have to tell me; don't tell me what you think you should have. Tell me what you want."

"In a perfect world?"

"Yes. In a perfect world, if you could wish for anything: what would your bridal shower look like?"

"No frills. No lacy crap."

I pretend to take notes on an imaginary clipboard with an air pen. "Gotcha. No frills, no lacy, no crap."

We giggle.

"I mean, I kind of want something fun and low-key, I'm just not sure exactly what that looks like."

"A brunch? A spa day?" I offer, "How about a night on the town?"

"I don't know," she says and then gets up to pitch her cup. "Come on, we've got to go back. I'll send you an email with all my contacts later."

"Fair enough," I pitch my cup too and follow her as we head back to work.

Sometime that afternoon, I need a break and log onto Facebook. Scrolling through various political rants and cute baby pictures, I come across a sponsored ad for a place called Cupcake City.

It sparks a thought, and once I Google and see exactly what they have to offer, I pick up the phone and give them a good old-fashioned call. A few minutes later, I have a page full of notes and a solid idea for Dez's bridal shower: Cupcake City offers a custom cupcake baking experience for up to thirty people which includes lunch, champagne, and of course the cupcakes we bake as dessert. I think this is right up Dez's alley, but before I buzz her with the idea, I call the shelter and ask to speak to Jazz.

Jazz is Dez's shelter friend; she's one of the executive directors of the domestic violence assistance program, and I know that she will want in on the new idea that just popped into my head.

"How about we bake a couple of batches of cupcakes, and then you can bring a whole slew of them back to share at the shelter after the shower?" I propose this knowing that Dez will love the idea, and that Jazz will be on board in less than a half second.

"Well, you don't have to twist my arm, girlfriend," Jazz responds with her trademark laugh, and I picture her smile, which could light up a skyscraper.

"I knew you'd love it," I'm starting to get excited. "I still have to get Dez on board but I think this type of shower may be just what she's looking for," I fill her in on all the details, and we hang up not long after, with promises to be in touch as we lead up to the event.

I buzz Dez, and within a few minutes she appears.

"Coffee?" She suggests.

I look at my watch. "I'm supposed to meet James in an hour, so I'll take a raincheck." I'm eager to tell her I figured it out. "Sit!"

"So what's up?" She plops down on the chair opposite me.

"I think I found your shower spot!" I fill her in on all the details, and as I'm talking, I see her nodding her head and smiling.

"I like it," she gives me a final nod. "I think it's perfect. You waste no time."

"I already contacted Jazz and she's in on the cupcake delivery," I pull out my trusty calendar and start looking at dates. "Pick a Saturday, any one but the day between Passover and Easter."

"Are you still thinking about taking on two holidays?" She gives me a significant eye roll.

"Mulling."

"Did James have his little conference with Uncle Ben yet?"

"Negative."

"And you are…?"

"Waiting in the wings."

"That must be hell for an uber-planner such as yourself," Dez casually observes.

"It's sort of like being in Purgatory."

"Hence the swift pace of the bridal shower planning," Dez adds.

"Well…"

"You have nothing, pal. I know you inside out."

"Well!" I try to control the smirky smile that is starting to make a profound appearance, but I cannot. She speaks the truth.

"Listen, let me talk to my mother, and Jack, and then we'll pick a date," Dez begins to unwind herself from my chair.

"Wait! You just want to talk to Jack about the date for his side, right? This isn't a Jack-and-Jill thing…correct?" I'm about to panic, thinking I misunderstood.

"No, it's a Jack and Dez thing," she laughs. "and there will be absolutely no men at my bridal shower."

"Gotcha."

Chapter Eighteen

Once Saturday rolls around, I am knocked out on the couch with a hot cup of tea and a desire to do anything but get in the shower and make my way over to Vivian and Vlad's.

"What's the chance we can stay here all day?" I realize it sounds like I'm whining, but I can't help myself, the blankets are warm, and my husband quite handsome.

"Let's say slim to none," James sighs. "And I know you're not in the mood to do me any favors, but any chance you can make some form of dessert that'll make the whole night tolerable?"

"I'm always in the mood to do you a favor," I counter. I place my tea on the table next to me and then not-so-gracefully lunge across the couch and fall on top of James.

"Ooof!" James laughs at my lack of grace and we snuggle up for a while, each of us lost in our own thoughts.

"How about mint chocolate chip cookies?" I suggest.

"I'm pretty sure those are Vlad's favorite. Sounds like a plan," James says as he repositions himself under me.

"You're welcome," I say, as I lift myself off the couch to go preheat the oven. "More tea?"

"Yes," James answers me as he clicks the television on, and I know I've lost him for at least a short while. It's okay; since I decided to make the cookies, I need to check and make sure I actually have all the ingredients on hand.

As I struggle to get all my ingredients out of my designated baking cabinet and onto the island, my phone pings, and I see that it's my Dad.

"Hey Dad!" I pick up and then lay out all my utensils. "Where have you been?" It seems as if we've been playing phone tag for weeks.

"Well, I've been in and out of town, and I just sat down and decided that it's time to call my favorite girl," he paused. "How have you been?"

"Great. Crazy. The usual." I fill him in on Aunt Bunny's diagnosis as I begin mixing. "We're headed to Vivian's tonight for dinner with David and his new girlfriend. In fact, I'm making cookies right now."

"Do they have any chocolate in them?" he asks.

"Well, I'm making mint chocolate chip, so I guess a bit... why?"

"You can hide a whole box of Ex-lax in a chocolate cake. I say you scrap the cookies, make a chocolate cake just for Vivian, and warn everyone else to stay away from it," he chuckles.

"Dad!" I hate to laugh at his evil idea, but I'm laughing.

"You know you'd love to. Hell, I bet you most days *Vlad* would love to!" He's laughing hard now, enjoying his joke.

"Well, I think I'm going to refrain...no matter how tempting it might be. These are actually Vlad's favorite." My eyes flick over to see James thoroughly involved in some financial show on TV, and I'm glad I didn't put my Dad on speaker.

"Anyway, I called to see what you guys are doing tomorrow, and if I can take you out to lunch?"

"Sure, why not? Let me double-check with James. Can I text you back?" I'm about done and would like to get the cookies in the oven so they have time to cool.

"Sure. Let me know and we'll go from there," he hesitates. "Have fun tonight!" He laughs again.

"Of course," I smile as I say it; glad he's in my corner. I put the phone down so that I can insert the cookies in the oven, tidy up a few things while I wait for the first batch to come out, then sit down and start making a list while the second batch is doing its thing.

I take a sheet of paper and write Passover on the left-hand side and then Easter on the right. I run to my junk drawer where I find a ruler and make a straight line down the center of the page. I decide I may as well begin to brainstorm some ideas; whether or not I host both holidays, I figure it'll be a good idea to get some plans in place and it always helps me to see my thoughts take shape on the page. I treat it like the start of a new ad campaign: I simply begin jotting down words on either side of the page, free-associating, so to speak. I plan as if I'm going to host, and then decide to do two drafts, just in case Aunt Bunny feels well enough to host Passover. I'm in the middle of plotting when the timer goes off for the second batch of cookies.

James hears the buzz and jumps off the couch, like Pavlov's dog, bounding into the kitchen.

"I heard you're giving out samples," he putters around the island sniffing and then decides which one has his name on it.

"Only for you, dear," I allow him one and then shoo him away when he attempts to palm another. "They're for everyone, you know."

"I know." He acts exasperated but I see the tug of a smile betray him.

"By the way, what time is good for lunch tomorrow? My father's around, and I told him we can meet up with him." I'm about to get in the shower and want to text him before I forget.

"Whatever you think," James hesitates. "Is it brunch or lunch?"

"Well, he said lunch…why, would you rather brunch?"

"No. I want to sleep in a little and not feel so rushed," he sighs. "I feel like we're going from one family thing to the next. What's the chance that you and I can get away next weekend? Just the two of us? No schedule…no nothing…but fun, of course?"

"Let's say slim to none," I wink at him, but I'm really not sure. "Let me check a few thousand things and get back to you."

"Deal."

$\mathcal{C}$hapter $\mathcal{N}$ineteen

By the time we make it over to Vivian and Vlad's house, the whole crew is already assembled, and it warms my heart to see Uncle Ben and Aunt Bunny laughing from the minute I walk through the door.

Jill and Ira are there as well, and I'm happy to see her once-coveted baby bump protruding nicely from her middle. Jill is the type of woman who is radiantly pregnant, and knowing how badly she ached for a child, I am actually looking forward to hearing about her journey thus far.

Once we've greeted everyone and filled our plates from the perennially-ordered platters, we settle around the table, and I find myself sitting next to David's new girlfriend Diana.

"So glad to finally meet you," I say before I shove some food in my mouth.

"You too," she smiles brightly, and seems normal, so I decide to engage her in conversation in between bites.

"I hear you're a police officer too?" I inquire with mild

interest, knowing that interest will fade quickly if she launches into a David-type tirade. David is the type of law enforcement officer that considers everyone a criminal; he's cop-talk all day long, and it's sometimes hard to take.

"Yes. I work for the Animal Cruelty Investigation Squad. It's tough work, but I love my job, and I love investigations. Being an animal lover makes my work that much easier."

Now this interests me. I am a huge animal advocate and often talk about getting a dog, but know full well that James and I are not home often enough to give a dog the love and attention that it deserves. I'm sure one day the right opportunity will come, but until then, I simply cry during ASPCA commercials and regularly stuff envelopes with checks written out to all types of different rescue organizations.

"How do you find out about animals being abused?" I'm curious about the process, and there's something about Diana that I automatically like, so I tune into her and tune out the rest of the clan.

"Well, there's the usual calls to 911 and such, but just this week, I got a call from a veterinarian that came across a stray in their parking lot. Once the vet tech got the dog to come inside, it was determined that the dog had been neglected for quite some time and quite possibly was dumped there." she shrugged, but unlike David, her face did the talking. "We decided to try and locate the owners, and at the same time, called up a local rescue to see if they could step in and find a better home for the pup. Right now it's still an active investigation."

"Does it tear your heart out?" I found myself getting choked up just hearing the story.

"Of course," she sighs. "But I remind myself every single day that I'm their advocate, and somehow, it gets me through."

"So how did you meet David?" By now my curiosity was piqued.

"David and I met at a fundraiser for a fellow officer whose son has been diagnosed with leukemia," Diana smiled at him from across the table. "He really knows how to bust a move!"

I practically spit out my salad. I have a picture in my head of David, dancing in full uniform, utility belt bouncing up and down. I'm sure that's not how they met, but my impression of David is that he's way too uptight to dance.

"Really?" I take a long drink and try to hide my incredulous smile behind the glass.

"Oh, you have no idea!" she whoops, obviously recalling dance floor shenanigans.

I decide right then and there that I like her...and I hope that she sticks around. We chat each other up for a while longer, and eventually I get up and make the rounds, visiting with Uncle Ben, Aunt Bunny, Jill and Ira, and even Vivian and Vlad.

"Thank you my dear, how did you know these were my favorite?" Vlad sidles up next to me as I open up the cookie tray in the kitchen. He steals a cookie and then waggles his eyebrows at me as he takes a bite and chews. "Mmmmmm."

"I think a little birdie told me." We both know he's the bird.

"Smart birdie," he responds by picking up another two cookies before I lift them off the counter and bring them into the dining area. As I place the cookies down, I notice that Vivian is nursing a Toasted Almond and interrogating Diana. I leave them be, sure that if Diana can handle both David and criminals; she can deal with the likes of Vivian.

I sashay over to James and join him on the couch. I force him to move in a bit and practically sit on top of him.

"Miss me?" I inquire while only half-joking, because even though we've been in the same house all night, we've barely said two words to one another.

"More than you realize," he whispers into my hair and I find myself feeling all warm and fuzzy. I stroke his collar and fit my hand under his arm, sitting next to him for a long moment, enjoying the warmth of his body and the comfortable silence as everyone around us makes lively conversation.

I decide right then to take a good, long look at my schedule and see what I can come up with; he's right about needing a weekend together, and I don't know if we can wait until Dez and Jack's wedding in order to have some time alone. A still small voice inside me tells me to feed my marriage, and in an effort to listen, I determine to make it happen. Until then, I get up, grab a couple of cookies, and feed my husband.

Chapter Twenty

James and I get as much sleep as possible, only to dash around the house and get ready quickly so that we can meet my Dad on time.

"So did you end up talking to Uncle Ben about the holidays?" I ask as I slam the passenger door to his car and start fastening my seat belt.

"Sort of; he wants to take a wait and see approach, and I told him that we're there to help either way." James looks at me out of the corner of his eye. "Are you going to be okay with that?"

I'm already preparing make-ahead meals in my head; thinking about what will freeze well and what I can make on the fly.

"That's fine," I nod my head to show I'm a team player.

"Okay. After lunch, can we perhaps synch our calendars and see if we have a whole weekend we can claim as our own?" James inquires.

"Sure," I don't know what else to say just yet, as I have a funny feeling that every weekend coming up has something, but I don't want to outright disappoint him. Team player...again.

After a few minutes more, we pull up into the parking lot of one of my Dad's favorite restaurants. It's a cozy café called Mimosa and I find myself craving exactly that as we get out of the car and enter the place.

I spy him already ensconced in his favorite banquette, waving to us as we pause at the hostess stand. When we cross the room to join him, I see a woman trailing me out of my peripheral vision and I move a few steps left so that she can pass.

"Sorry," I smile at her.

Imagine my surprise when my father jumps up and invites her to sit on an inside seat right next to him. I pause and stare at him, unsure of what exactly is happening.

"Rhonda, James! This is Julia. I invited her to come have lunch with us," my father begins blushing profusely and waving his hands as he speaks, "...come! Sit!" He gestures towards the other side of the booth, and I hear James making introductions as I am left trying to figure out exactly where I know this woman from.

By the time we're shaking hands, it occurs to me that she is the same woman I met at the coffee shop, with the blindingly white teeth and the eager smile.

"Nice to see you again," I recover as best I can, painfully aware of the fact that she's not much older than me. And she's gushing all over my father. I feel my heart start beating triple time, and as I glance at James, I know he knows exactly how I feel.

At least there's that.

It takes a few more minutes to recover from this nonchalant ambush, but I bury my head in the menu and make all the right noises as the three of them make small talk. Eventually, I begin calming down, and at the same time, find myself wondering if it would be strange to start using Pilates-style breaths at the table.

Thankfully, the server comes over and offers us a Mimosa Menu: this is a one-page list of different mimosa concoctions, and I decide to order the tropical, which is made with pineapple juice instead of orange.

"That sounds great! I'll have one too!" Julia exclaims.

"Me three," a jovial man masquerading as my father actually winks at her before handing the list back to the server.

James orders something totally different and squeezes my knee under the table.

For this I am grateful.

"So!" My father, trying too hard, launches into a funny story about something that happened to him recently at work. Apparently, Julia works on the client side of his business and feels comfortable interjecting here and there. I watch this awkward ballet all while trying to keep an open mind.

By the time we're ready to make decisions about dessert; I'm settling into the conversation a bit more and trying to focus on the people at the table. I find that I'm not upset about my father dating this woman...I just don't understand why he was hiding it from me. Could it be her age? I'm not exactly sure where to place her, but I'd hazard a guess that Julia is somewhere in her forties, and that would make her only about ten or so years older than me.

It would also make her about ten or so years younger than him. Of course, that's none of my business, but I find that I'm put off more by the way he introduced her than the fact that she's here. The truth is that although my father has dated some since my mother passed away, they've all been older, grandmotherly-type women who never stuck around long enough to warrant an afternoon at Mimosa. Did that mean that this is serious? Had they been together for a while already? Was this really the best way for him to introduce this new person into our lives?

Even though the questions were piling up inside my heart, I chose to continue to play nice and order a salted caramel brownie.

Because God knows I needed one.

Chapter Twenty-One

I'm waving and smiling but my teeth are clenched, and I wait for the door to shut fully and the engine to be turned on before I turn to James and ask, "What the hell was that?"

"My guess is your father has a new girlfriend," James says.

"No kidding, Einstein! I mean, what was with the ambush? Why didn't he let me know in advance that he was dating someone who would actually understand all my cultural references and quite possibly grew up watching all the same television shows?" I feel as if I've been holding my tongue for more than a couple of hours.

"Yes, I kind of got the picture that she was a bit younger than him," James responds.

"You think?" I shake my head and stare at him as if he's an alien creature. "I mean...I don't mind, I want him to be happy, but...what the hell was that?" I gesture, but it's a flailing of arms of sorts, and I realize that there are a million things I want to say, but I have to organize my thoughts.

"Let me ask you something," James grabs my hand as he maneuvers the car, "Did you father ever give you a hard time about us?"

"How so?" I'm not following.

"Well, look…maybe your father didn't want you to marry a Jewish guy? Maybe to him, in a perfect world, it would have been easier if I had come wrapped up in a different sort of package," he shrugs.

"What do you mean?" I protest, "My father loves you! He has always liked, and then loved you…he has not once given me a hard time about you!" I find myself appalled and not sure where this conversation is headed.

"Fine, but what if he had reservations, and just didn't share them with you?"

"You mean, the way Vivian finds it okay to constantly share her reservations out loud, in a room full of people?" I can almost feel the smoke coming out of my ears and I'm starting to crack open the window.

"Rhonda, you know what? That was unnecessary. How did Vivian suddenly jump right into the picture?"

"Because she jumps right into everything?" I suggest.

"Fine. Fine! But I'm talking about your Dad here, and your expectations, and your *'shoulds'* and the fact that maybe you need to look at that," he sighs heavily as he parks the car and we make our way into our house.

"Well, maybe you need to look at the fact that Julia With the Big Teeth doesn't yet need an under-eye cream, and that perhaps I was just a little put off by the fact that I have colleagues her age and that THEY ARE HAPPILY MARRIED AND RAISING

SMALL CHILDREN, NOT RUNNING AROUND WITH A MAN WHO JUST RECEIVED HIS AARP CARD IN THE MAIL!" I hear myself shouting but I can't seem to stop, and I realize all of the sudden that I no longer want to even look at James.

"Hoo boy," James shrugs off his coat and turns to me but I stalk past him and slam the door to our bedroom.

He doesn't follow.

I sit on the bed and feel as if I want to cry, but I don't really know why. It's not like I didn't like Julia; she was nice enough and was able to carry on a good conversation. Perhaps I didn't like the idea that my father seemed to be totally enamored with her...? I toss that idea aside and decide right then and there that I need some fresh air. I change quickly from brunch clothes into lined yoga pants and a couple of sweatshirts; it's not Spring yet, but not freezing either. I lace up my sneakers and decide to take off and perhaps cool down. Once I exit the bedroom, James looks up from the couch and simply nods his head.

"I'll be back," I say, and then I leave and find myself outside, not too sure of where I'm headed. I start off down our street and then decide to head to the nearest high school and take a few laps around the track. I'm walking, not running, but I feel better once I'm moving and I know that I'll need to apologize to James for overreacting. I hate the fact that I get like this, but it seems as if marriage does this to people, and still being kind of new at it, I'm not quite sure why.

Is it that old adage that we hurt the ones we love the most? Did we take things out on each other the same way when we were still dating? I think about it for a while, but after a few laps around the track, I can't say for sure. I think about what James said about getting away for a weekend, and although I know it will help, I still haven't given my calendar a serious look and I'm not really sure why.

I walk until I don't want to walk anymore and then I head home realizing I lost track of how many laps I did, not caring either way. I hate this feeling that seems as if it's poisoning every piece of my life it comes into contact with, this feeling of unease, this escalating fear that keeps screaming in my ear about all the things I can't control. I don't know what to do for now so I let myself back in and find James snoring on the couch, a basketball game still playing on the television. I leave him be and take a long, hot shower. When I get out, nothing is solved, but I feel better.

Chapter Twenty-Two

"So did you kiss and make up?" Dez is inquiring with the tenacity of Oprah Winfrey, and I feel like jumping off the couch.

"Yes! Yes, we did…it's just…" I trail off here.

"Just what?" she prods.

"Just everything," which I know is not a response.

"Rhonda," she breathes, "It's change. You hate change. Face it: it's change, the unknown…the stuff you can't plan or make a little chart for…" She gives me the ta-da face.

"Well, that's not fair." I'm pouting; fully aware of the pouting.

"Maybe not, but it's accurate. Listen: there's nothing you can do about anybody else's crap but your own. Look at my mother! I can't begin to tell you how many times I would have rearranged her life if I could–killed the jerk she was married to and disposed of the body–but eventually I figured out that the only person I could control was me," Dez pointed to her heart. "I wish I could give you that."

"I know that." I sound insistent, yet we both know that she's better at it than I will ever be. The mere fact that Dez has blown off her entire family every Christmas since I've known her speaks volumes as to the stark stylistic contrast between us. And in that instance she was not only right, but in the right place at the right time, because by following her heart and volunteering at the shelter...she met Jack and the rest is history.

"Let's head back," Dez suggests, so we clean up our stuff and start heading back to work. "I think Artie wants to see some ideas at three."

I groan because I know that none of us are ready. The entire team was hashing it out in the conference room earlier today, trying to figure out what flavors would work for the Perfect Protein brand and at the same time what flavors would make people want to participate in a contest. By the time we broke for lunch, we felt as if we had done a whole lot of nothing.

"I'll see you later," I say to Dez as we part at the elevator. I have to go back to my desk and take care of some general house-keeping, and I decide to try and rein in my clutter again; it's amazing to me how I can be so utterly organized and yet my desk continuously slides into a slow decline every time I turn around.

I flick on some serious jazz, close the door, and begin to take care of the one thing that's in my control. While I'm sorting and shredding, my mind is still playing with the different threads of ideas we have for this new ad campaign, but I find I'm not in love with any of them. By the time Dez buzzes me for the meeting I'm still in tumult, and when I enter the conference room, the noise level is just short of deafening.

"Who likes coconut ANYTHING?" Ramon is pontificating

and at the same time gesturing wildly with a water bottle in his left hand. "I can vividly recall pulling anything with coconut out of my Halloween bag like the plague that it was, and handing it off to anyone who would eat it. Almond Joy? Almond Misery is what I say!"

I say a quick prayer that his water bottle is capped properly, or we're all about to have a quick shower.

"That's your opinion," Lola counters with a face that is silently pleading with the rest of us for some form of rescue. "There is a huge portion of the world that likes coconut; people *actually* enjoy it. For some people: ALMOND ENJOY! Get it? Ever hear of the Coconut Water Craze?! I think we should capitalize on that, especially because people who drink coconut water and eat protein bars are generally healthy."

I catch Dez's eye and we share a glance that says we are both proud and amazed, as Lola usually isn't as vocal as Ramon.

"Well, I've got some stuff up on the whiteboard already, so let's just continue until Artie gets here," Alex suggests with a quick glance to his watch.

"Okay, are we all at least on the same page with the three different flavors?" Dez opens this up to the group. "Lola seems to be familiar with, and likes, the M&M model...so let's work with that for now, and see what we come up with."

Soon we're all proposing different flavor combinations, some ridiculous, some not. By 3:30, Artie has entered the room and basically sits in the back and observes, offering nothing initially.

"I think the coconut thing sucks," Artie finally joins the conversation.

"BAM! Thank YOU!" Ramon is ecstatic.

I'm feeling for Lola, so I interject with, "But I do see the correlation that Lola's trying to make."

"Fine," Artie says, but his face says *not fine.* "Were you also the little girl who *liked* getting the infamous box of raisins in her treat bag on Halloween?" He makes a barfing gesture.

"Well..." I trail off here.

"I think she's the one who talked about Rum Raisin," Ramon is on a tear, outing me with unabashed glee.

"Well!" I'm blushing now.

"Look!" Artie finally gets up to command the stage. "Look eye!" Artie does this weird thing with his fingers pointing towards the table and then directly towards his eyes. He doesn't stop until everyone is looking directly at him and there's silence in the room.

He summons us with this iconic gesture, then blanches. "I don't eat protein bars, so I can honestly care less, but we need to get moving on this thing. Alex, can you get Seth to work with you on the storyboards, and Lola: can you take the lead on the flavor angle, since you've actually liked the M&M page on social media?" He makes a face as if to indicate this is strange.

"And can I just add that nobody wants double anything?" Ramon throws this out, apropos of nothing.

"What?" I look at him as if he's finally lost it.

"What I'm saying here is," and he basically glares in Lola's direction, "if someone likes coconut water, that doesn't necessarily mean that they also want a coconut protein bar to go along with it!"

"No doubles," Alex writes this on the white board as if it's something of note.

"Okay! Let's go!" Artie begins gesturing towards the door. "Now, off you go to FORM, STORM, NORM, and PERFORM!"

Dez and I share a glance as we leave, and I know if nothing else I've got my work cut out for me. I sigh as I return to my desk, and try to bury myself in the mundane while waiting for lightning to strike.

Chapter Twenty-Three

"Okay, well…I've got a dress fitting with Dez next weekend, and then the weekend after that…I'm supposed to be getting together with Amalia, Valentina, Jazz, and Dez to work on party favors for the shower…" I trail off here, skip ahead a bit in my calendar, but every weekend has something scribbled on it for the next few weeks at least.

"I figured as much," James pulls a face and then takes a long sip of his beer. We're sitting on the floor, mediocre Chinese take-out splayed across the coffee table, each of us with our calendars out and pens at the ready.

"I'm sorry babe." And I find that I sincerely am, wishing we could make time for a solid weekend alone. "But the good news is that we only have a couple of months to May, and if you want to, we can extend our vacation a little and spend some quality time in St. Lucia."

"I love the idea of that; I'm just wondering if Dez and Jack will want us tagging along for their entire honeymoon," He muses.

"I can ask."

"Well, let's see. Tomorrow is Aunt Bunny's surgery, so we're probably better off sticking around right now anyway."

"Ah, yes! I decided to make stuffed shells."

"With the spinach?"

"Yes, with the spinach tucked inside, just the way you like it."

"You're the best."

"I try," I wince as I say it. Lately, there's been this unspoken thing of trying to be all things to all people bubbling up inside me, and I'm finding it both exhausting and off-putting. I haven't exactly given voice to it yet–not even with James–and I feel as if I'm still working it out in my head. And heart.

As for right now, I'm content to cuddle with James on the couch and contemplate a wine-braised beef brisket for Passover. A lovely woman named Helene in our reception area at work gave me the recipe last year around Passover but I didn't attempt to make it since Aunt Bunny did her usual spread. I'm starting to wonder if I should give her recipe a trial run, just in case Aunt Bunny doesn't feel well enough to host...and an instant later I tell myself to stop. We don't know anything yet, and I don't want to get ahead of myself.

My mind flicks to the party favors that Dez suggested: chocolate covered pretzels for a takeaway. Amalia has been trying to talk her out of them because we're making cupcakes, but I told her to go for it–they're Jack's favorite, and people never mind taking home something consumable. It's the tchotchkes that nobody wants anymore; what the hell are you supposed to do with a dinner bell with someone else's name on it? I can still remember uncovering about a dozen of those one day in my mother's china cabinet and wondering why she held onto them.

Of course, the thoughts about my mother led me right to thinking about my father and his new-found friend. I never did hear from him after our lunch, which leads me to believe that all is right in his world, and that he has no idea that I'm even the least bit upset or concerned about him. The question I keep asking myself is this: is it even worth mentioning? I don't want there to be this strange feeling of unease between us and I certainly don't want to rain on his parade.

I continue to cuddle with James on the couch, and as my mind continues to run off in a thousand different directions, I sincerely wonder why it can't run in the direction of a great ad campaign. Whenever I'm outside of work lately, I feel as if my mind won't shut down, and yet when I'm at work, I feel as if I can't seem to string together cohesive thoughts, and I'm finding myself grasping at straws. I'm not even clear on what exactly we're supposed to be doing with the flavor campaign. Are we asking people to vote on their favorite flavor? And then what? For some reason, this approach feels off to me, but I can't quite discern why, at least not yet.

James interrupts my endless noodling then with a simple question that I don't hear.

"I'm sorry, what did you say?" I raise my head off his shoulder and look him square in the face.

"Are you ready to clean up and head to bed? I'm starting to yawn and my arm's falling asleep," he nods his head to the side I'm lying on.

"Sure," I untangle myself and begin cleaning up the debris. I stack the calendars one on top of the other on our kitchen island,

and James takes care of the recyclables. In just a few minutes, we're headed for bed, and I wonder if my mind will finally shut down and allow me to sleep. Tomorrow is a big day. I cross my fingers and pray and at some point about an hour later, I look at the clock one last time and give into sleep.

Chapter Twenty-Four

"What time is it?" James mutters to himself (or me) and then turns over in an attempt to fall back asleep.

Thankfully, I set two alarms.

That way, when the second alarm goes off ten minutes later, I not only bolt straight out of bed myself, but am able to shake him awake and somehow orchestrate the morning routine. By the time he gets out of the shower, I have a thermos filled with his favorite coffee and leave him a sack full of Perfect Protein bars for a quick something on the way to the hospital. I was due for an early meeting at work and was going to meet up with them later on, bringing food along for Uncle Ben and whoever else showed up. Once James left, I hurry up and am out the door just a few minutes behind him, my mind running as fast as my feet. As soon as I get to work, I find the day filled with a meeting that wasn't necessary, endless emails to return, an incessantly ringing phone, and eventually a full-on headache. I was about to raise the proverbial white flag when Dez stuck her head in my office.

"Anything yet?" She was as concerned about Aunt Bunny as the rest of us, and I love her for it.

"Not yet. I keep checking my phone, but James only texted me once so far and let me know he was there and that Uncle Ben seemed to be holding up okay," I let out a big breath. "I thought I would have heard something more by now."

I had barely finished my sentence when I hear a ping and look over to check my phone. James is finally texting me, but he must have hit enter too soon. I found myself tapping my desk as I waited for the little bubbles to produce more actual words.

Dez hung on the door, waiting.

"Ah. He says that the surgeon just met with Uncle Ben and that they think the operation was successful; they're going to hang out there for a while longer as the doctor may want to release her today." I shrugged. "I think that's as good as it gets."

"What can I do for you?" Dez nodded towards me.

"A double espresso?" I wasn't sure whether coffee would help or hurt the headache situation, but I was willing to try.

"You got it. Let me grab my bag and my phone and I'll meet you by the elevators," With that, Dez disappears. I grab my stuff and just a few minutes later, I'm sipping a coffee and making a strange sigh of Ahhh…as if I hadn't had one in years.

"What is it about a hot beverage that makes everything else almost tolerable?" I muse out loud.

"It's like soup. You're sick: you want soup. A horrible commute? Soup. Depressed? Soup. It's hot and slurpy and it gets the job done." Dez says.

"When I'm depressed I want brownies."

"Brownies and soup."

"Not together though."

"No, of course not."

We share a smile and I slurp my coffee, comforted by the banter that I needed, without even knowing that I needed it.

"I miss Uncle Ben." I start to cry now, tears that I didn't see coming, and I find myself surprised by the words that just popped out of my mouth.

"What do you mean?" Dez puts her hand on my knee and allows me to sniff and try and regain my composure.

"It's strange, right? But I haven't had a whole lot of one-on-one time with him since the beginning of Aunt Bunny's diagnosis. I feel like everyone's been trying to be there for him, for them, and I keep trying–unconsciously or subconsciously–to give him space, and let everyone else step in and comfort him. I've just been trying to keep all the balls in the air, and I can't remember the last time I connected with him one on one," I take a deep breath and shake my head. "It sounds like a stupid thing to be concerned with right now."

"I think it's what's surfacing," Dez offers me a loving smile. "I think when you see him tonight you need to give him a great big hug. For him and for you."

"I will," I promise her and myself. Eventually, I hoist myself up off the chair and collect myself enough to go finish the day at work. I've already decided that not a whole lot is going to get done today; my mind is still shuffling and nothing is clear. I go back to work and start playing at getting organized, but I eventually give in and decide to leave and go meet James and Uncle Ben. I text them on the way out the door, only to find out that they're releasing Aunt Bunny and that everyone is headed over to their house.

I take that as my cue, so I run home to change and grab the stuffed shells, chicken soup, and blackout banana bread that I made especially for Uncle Ben. Once my car is loaded up, I double back inside to grab a bottle of wine, then make my way over there as quickly as possible. I arrive to find only James and Uncle Ben sitting in the den, with no sign of Vivian or anyone else.

"Did I miss everyone?" I feel conflicted: happy that I don't have to deal with Vivian tonight, and sad because I somehow feel like I missed something.

"I told Vivian to go home," Uncle Ben makes a sound which would normally include an eye roll and a bit of laughter, but his eyes look tired, and I seize the opportunity to hug him right then and there. I hold him close for a long moment and end our embrace with an extra squeeze. I've missed him; the twinkle in his eye and our usual repartee seem to be on hiatus, but I pray that it's only temporary as I let him go and insist that they let me feed them.

"My God, you made enough food for an Army!" James seems surprised.

"You should know better," I say lovingly as he looks pretty wiped too. "I'd rather have too much than not enough."

"Of course," James puts his arms around me from behind as I begin dishing out the shells. "Thanks, babe."

I feel his warm breath on my shoulder and after lifting the first plate into the microwave, I turn around and give him a big hug too. "I brought some wine."

"That you didn't need to do," Uncle Ben says, "because I always have enough wine for an Army!"

We all chuckle, and as the first plate beeps ready, I hand it off to James. We work together and in less than five minutes, we're all seated and eating. Though the conversation is minimal, there's a comfortable silence, and I find my mind settling down for the first time all day. I realize there's not much I can do right now: Aunt Bunny is sleeping, James and Uncle Ben are eating their first real meal of the day, and I also find that I am okay with not doing much at all. I have a fleeting thought that maybe that's the kind of love I need to practice more often; a love that can simply be, and does not have to actively try so hard all the time.

I take a sip of the wine the guys opened and in the ensuing silence, I polish off the rest of my plate.

"Who's up for some banana blackout bread?" I offer, knowing that Uncle Ben will be happy to demolish a generous piece. Once I slice three generous pieces, I begin wrapping up the leftovers as I take a bite. It's the kind of comfort food that's necessary at times like these: old-school banana bread loaded with chocolate, and in the process of cleaning up, I think about Dez's comment regarding brownies and soup, and it makes my heart smile.

Close enough.

Chapter Twenty-Five

"Dad!" I exclaim as I hear his voice on the other end of the phone. Although I automatically look at the Caller ID whenever I pick up the phone, this time I grabbed it without even a glance, expecting it to be James.

"Rhonda!" he mimics me with a laugh in his voice.

"Sorry, Dad, I just assumed it was James," I offer as I start powering down my computer and grabbing all the items I think I may need to grab before closing up shop.

"No worries," he says. "So how have you been? I haven't heard from you since Mimosa."

"I...ah..." I grab the sweater that comes to the office with me every week, only to get toted back home unworn, and a small part of my brain wonders why I continuously do this even as I try to focus on the call. "I've been so busy!" I fill him in quickly with a short list of everything's that's been going on.

"So how's Bunny?" he inquires.

"I think she's going to be okay. Her doctor ordered up a few visits with a PT for her to do some arm exercises and they're managing whatever pain and discomfort she's having, but the prognosis is good, and I think we'll all breathe easier as time passes," I find myself exhaling.

"That's good news. She's a doll. I still have no idea how she and Vivian are related," he guffaws.

I try not to laugh, but his humor always makes me smile, no matter how inappropriately timed his remarks can be.

"Well, I still have no idea how Vivian and James are related," I add in, much to his delight.

"Listen, kiddo...I realized after I introduced you to Julia that maybe I should have told you about her beforehand." His abrupt change of subject catches me off guard. That's twice in one conversation.

"It's..." I trail off here, trying to choose my words wisely. "It's not a problem, Dad, I was just a little surprised by her..."

"Youthful glow?" He chuckles.

"Well, yes, I..."

"I get it," he sighs, "Listen kiddo, I thought about that after the fact. The truth is, she's into a lot of the same things I'm into, and where it goes from here is anybody's guess." He laughs again, this time a full-out laugh, "She makes me laugh."

"And isn't that the most important thing?" I don't know what else to say here, and besides, I do believe that it's important to be with someone who can make you laugh.

"Right now it is," he responds, then changes the subject as abruptly as he started it. "So what are you doing for Easter?"

"Well, I was thinking the usual suspects for a casual brunch. Why? Do you guys want to come?" I'm hoping he says both yes and no.

"Sure," he slides into it. "Let me know what time and I'll be there. By the way, when's Passover?"

"It starts Good Friday night this year," I say, "And you're welcome to come to that too; we're just not sure who's doing what yet because usually Aunt Bunny and Uncle Ben host."

"Gotcha. Okay, I'll be in touch." With that, he rings off.

I stuff the sweater in my bag and go. I'm meeting James at our favorite bistro, and after that, I'm hoping to go home and pass out. Such elaborate plans for a Friday night.

By the time I enter the bistro, James has our table reserved and I see him chatting up our favorite waiter; it's this simple rhythm of our days and nights that bring me comfort, and I find myself looking forward to the many years that stretch out ahead of us.

"Hey there," I greet him with a smile and a swift kiss, taking my seat opposite him.

"Hey there to you," he responds with a casual once-over and I wonder briefly if I've spilled something on my shirt.

"How was your day?" I begin, looking directly at him while pushing away the menu. I pretty much know what we're ordering, and either way, I'm not sure I care.

"Tiring. Annoying. Not exactly a banner day, but not a bad one either. And yours?" he asks politely.

"It was a day. I'm happy that it's Friday. Please tell me we can sleep in tomorrow," I cast a pleading eye his way.

"We certainly can," he smiles now, the genuine smile that I love, and I return the favor. "In fact, I am going to be…ah, recharging my phone. All morning," he adds, and I can't help but perk up a bit.

"Oh good; so am I," I demure.

Chapter Twenty-Six

"Keep in mind that it's exactly what I would have picked whether I was getting married at the beach or in a ballroom," Dez reminds me, "and that's the only reason that I didn't try on 756 dresses."

"756? Is that an arbitrary number, or were you shooting for it?" I have to give her at least a little bit of a hard time.

"It's a very special number," Dez tries to insist this with a straight face but we both end up laughing. We're walking to the Bridal Shop where she got her dress, and from there we're off to try and find me something stunning at the high-end department store we love. In an effort to not make me look like a typical maid of honor, Dez insisted that I pick out a dress I like, that fits great, and that I feel good in, with little to no other parameters. In some ways this has made dress shopping easy, and in some ways, incredibly difficult. This is why I insisted upon her company today as I browse. I'm pretty excited because they have an amazing evening wear section, and I've been known to wander the aisles from time to time, looking for an excuse to buy something covered with glitter.

Once she appears from behind the curtain in the dressing area, I find myself getting more than a little bit choked up; she's right. This dress is hers, and she owns it, no matter the venue.

"You look stunning," I shake my head and then clear my throat, hoping that I can keep it all together for my friend.

"Awww...stop that!" Dez glares at me, but she's smiling too, and we're both trying hard not to laugh. Dez is nothing if not her own person, and although I know she doesn't need anyone's approval, she's got mine, unequivocally.

"Did Amalia see it yet?" I ask this knowing their relationship, not sure of how much Dez is allowing her mother into this part of her journey.

"Not yet," Dez bites her lip and then adds, "I needed to do this on my own."

"I got you," I nod my approval.

Several turns and a few more pins and we're off to look for something for me. We start with a few New York staples: black cocktail dresses perfect for an evening wedding. Once I try on a couple, I realize that they aren't quite right for St. Lucia, so we split up and broaden our horizons. About a half hour later, we end up back at the dressing rooms with the same dress in hand.

"Well, I think I know which one's a finalist!" I exclaim.

"You're going to look great in green." She thrusts hers into my hands and I notice it's a size smaller than the one I picked up.

This is a sign of true friendship.

I try on a handful of dresses, leaving the uncharacteristic green for last, and know that we're both right the minute I slide it down my hips. Unfortunately, I'm more accurate than Dez in the size department, but I decide at that moment to cut my losses and call it a victory.

"The great thing about this dress is that I'll be able to eat in it," I declare an hour later when we stop to order drinks and a snack.

"That and you can wear it with sandals or pumps," Dez points out. "I'm actually thinking gold sandals…and I found these screaming blue, *hot* high heels, although I may just want to wear those later on for dancing."

"That sounds like a plan," I agree as we clink glasses and smile. I feel happy to have crossed one thing off my endless to-do list, and I savor the idea of having it all wrapped up by the time we hit the beach.

On the way home, I allow my mind to wander a bit, picturing myself and James hanging onto a float in the water, balancing tropical drinks with mini umbrellas sticking out of them, completely relaxed and enjoying the sun, sand, and each other.

Chapter Twenty-Seven

"Did you get that email?" I burst into Dez's office.

"Yes. I don't know whether he's having a nervous breakdown or doing cocaine, but something's up." Dez shakes her head and looks at me. "We've got a half an hour. Let's go get a coffee now, because it seems like we're going to need one."

As we're escaping to our caffeine haven downstairs in order to fuel up for our emergency meeting, I hear a buzz building in the hall. Everybody seems to be whispering about something. Dez and I exchange a glance; although Artie lends himself to drama, it's not often that he sends out an email like this one, and I can't remember the last time he called an emergency meeting.

By the time we're back people are shuffling into the conference room. I've barely claimed my chair when Artie breezes in, face stern, and takes his place at the front of the room.

"Listen. I need everyone's attention, and I need it fast. I wouldn't have called this meeting if we weren't up the creek without the proverbial paddle. Everybody get me?" He zeroes in on Ramon and does his infamous look/eye gesture.

The energy of the room is crackling with nerves.

"It is as simple and as complicated as this," he proceeds with an unhappy look on his face, "The CEO of Splash Beverages called me this morning."

He pauses.

Splash Beverages was the last big campaign that Dez and I worked on with this same team; we came up with a killer campaign–with a little help from Uncle Ben–and to this day, they remain the ad agency's biggest client.

"He made it incredibly clear that he doesn't want us investing any more time on Perfect Protein. In case you weren't aware: when Splash got into the sports drink market late last year, they acquired Perfect Protein as well. They are hoping to bombard the NBA this season with relentless marketing of all their products. That said: we need to wrap up Perfect Protein laser fast, and be ready to present it to them ten days from today. And by the way, for those of you who are wondering... they are not at all into the flavor contest thing. They want a different angle, and they made it crystal clear to me that if we don't deliver PP, we lose Splash."

There is utter silence in the room as each team member let that last sentence sink in.

"Exactly." Artie nods. "Looking at your faces, I can see that you're all beginning to get the gravity of the situation here. They're not playing, and this whole situation won't only affect the ad agency as a whole, but your individual livelihoods as well...if you get what I'm saying," he sighs, then rips his fingers through his hair. "What do we have so far?"

From silence, we all start talking over each other, and eventually Artie holds up a hand and yells, "Stop!"

We stop.

"Listen, I'm supposed to be out of town, but I'm not going anywhere while we're not getting anywhere." He waves his hands around. "So let's tidy up our other stuff, meet back here in a bit to brainstorm some more, then call it a night. Hopefully someone will have an overnight epiphany. Barring that, plan on staying late tomorrow, and all week, for as long as we need to...I'll buy dinner. They want it fast and fabulous, so let's give it to them!"

We're all in our own heads as we shuffle out, but just as I'm about to cross the threshold back into the hallway, Artie calls back me and Dez.

"I know you two already know this, but because you're the leads on Splash, if we lose that account..." he trails off, suddenly unable to make eye contact.

"We get it," Dez nods her head and turns on her heel.

I follow, my mind spinning, wondering how I'm going to create anything while I'm worried about keeping my job.

Chapter Twenty-Eight

When I get home later, I'm thrilled to see that James took care of dinner; there is simply no way I could've taken care of making an actual meal tonight.

"It's all going to work out," James insists. "Don't worry."

"I'm trying hard not to worry, but I'm not just worried for me. I'm worried for everyone. I don't want to see Dez lose her job right before her wedding. I know that you and I will be okay for a time; you can carry the mortgage, and I have a ton of contacts in the industry. It's just that..." I take a deep breath and continue, "as much as we all tend to bitch: I love my job. I love my team, and I love working with Dez, and I even love Artie."

"I get it," He's standing behind me as I begin to clear the plates, and I stop for an impromptu shoulder rub, "I totally get it."

"Thanks," I whisper as I continue to clean up, but my throat is tight and I'm not really sure why I'm being so emotional. It's not over yet. Who's to say that we won't suddenly come up with an amazing campaign? It's possible. It's still possible.

The problem is that it doesn't feel that way. From the very beginning, this campaign has felt heavy and redundant, and there haven't been any sparks flying throughout the room like there are sometimes when we all get together and work on a product. If I take a minute and get brutally honest with myself, I can admit that I have little to no interest in this particular campaign; I've been distracted by family issues, and everything feels like it's off beat.

After we load the dishwasher, I pick up the phone to check in on Uncle Ben. He sounds tired but says both he and Aunt Bunny are doing okay. I tell him that I am sending James over tomorrow night with food, and that I'll see him soon.

I write a note out for James, reminding him in bright red marker to take a tray from the freezer before heading to Uncle Ben's tomorrow night. I tidy up and then decide I need to get some sleep. Who knows what the rest of the week will bring. All I know is that I need to be fresh, and at the same time, I long for a serious escape. I opt for a favorite author's latest book, and the next thing I know, I'm deep into dreams.

Chapter Twenty-Nine

"I still don't get why they don't like the flavor contest," Lola sighs.

It's been three days and we're all out of ideas. I knew we would revisit this soon, but it still feels too soon.

"Nobody likes the flavor contest," Ramon rolls his eyes.

"I just think it's too long-term. Artie says they want something fast and fabulous," I try to be kind, or at least, kinder than Ramon.

"Well, I think we need to focus on the NBA," Alex throws this out there at the same time he throws a wadded up piece of paper in the air.

"The NBA games aren't the only place they're going to advertise," Dez points out, and we all sigh, because she's right.

"Okay, let's take twenty!" Artie claps his hands together. "We've got a few things up on the board. We'll stretch, grab a drink, and who knows, maybe something will pop out at us."

We all get up and go our separate ways, desperate to be away from forced creativity and unrealistic deadlines. I run to the bathroom, check my phone, and pace. I'm wearing a hole in the carpet by my desk when Dez puts her head in and intones, "We have to go back."

"Ugh!" I grab my things and trudge back over to the conference room.

"Sure, if we focus on how much protein each bar has, it'll speak to the hearts of every athlete out there," Alex is pontificating as we come back in, "but do you honestly check the grams of protein before you buy a bar?"

"I check the sugar," Dez says as she starts to sit down again.

"I pick a flavor I like," Lola puts in while giving Ramon the side-eye. He ignores her, tapping his pen on the table to an imaginary tune.

"I think the question we need to answer here is *why* does someone need this product?" Artie points out the obvious. "I mean, I don't eat the things, so…?" He opens this up to the room.

My mind flutters back to a couple of weeks ago, when James devoured one on the way to church.

"I think people eat them because they're convenient," I start, and then rise up out of the chair I just sat in. For the very first time since we began working on this product, it begins to click, and I begin to pace. "Look, no one would choose a protein bar over real food, but you can't exactly eat lasagna while driving."

Everybody laughs at the visual, but I'm on a roll, so I keep going.

"They're the thing that tides you over. They're portable. They're healthier than a candy bar. They're convenient," I'm repeating myself now as I pick up the pace and work along the length of the conference table. "What if we highlight that?"

"I see where you're going," Dez begins to nod, and I know she's following. "Screw the flavors, or even the grams of whatever...it's the packability that we need to talk about."

"You want NBA?" I turn to Alex. "Let's show an NBA player grabbing one of these three minutes before a game."

"Or a Mom with her hands full..." Dez offers.

"Or a guy, driving in his car, late to church, a meeting... whatever...knowing he's not going to be able to grab a bite for a while..." I'm picturing the scenarios we could offer, gesturing wildly with my hands. "How about this: 'When I want food, I crave Mom's pasta. But when I'm on the go, these are perfect.'"

"Good to go?" Ramon throws this out. "Or is that overused?"

"Hang onto it. I think we're finally getting somewhere," Artie begins pacing opposite me. "I like it...I like what I'm hearing...I could love it...let's keep it flowing, people!"

From that moment on, we're all in on the concept, and we spend the next couple of hours talking about the different scenarios we can portray. We decide to go real-life, relatable, and maybe funny: the guy stuck in traffic, desperate for a bite of anything, finds a Perfect Protein bar stuck in his center console and yells out: PERFECT!

The Mom who is maneuvering a double stroller, hands full of half-empty kiddie pouches turns to realize both kids are sleeping; she collapses on a nearby bench and pulls a bar out of a diaper bag: PERFECT.

The NBA star who's late getting to the arena and now has to get out there and win the playoff game: he grabs a bar from the mascot on the way out onto the court, and then we see a fabulous shot with the words PERFECT on the scoreboard. Maybe an over-the-shoulder wink at the mascot, or a kid in the stands, devouring a Perfect Protein bar.

We work through dinner, and finally pack it in when we have about thirty different scenarios on the board and enough for Alex and the rest of the artists to start creating storyboards that we can present to the client. We still need a tag line, but Artie finally calls it a day, and we agree that it's best to go home and get some rest so that we can come in and start fresh in the morning.

As I pull into the driveway, I see that James is home, but with no lights on, I assume he's sleeping. Just as I'm about to close the garage door, I catch my nosy neighbor Celia waving from over the hedge. She's got two dogs with her and she looks to be in some sort of a fluorescent vest.

"Hey Celia," I call, pausing as I go to hit the button for the garage door.

"Hello Rhonda!" She's breathing heavy. "You see what I've got here? This here's a bag full of JWAP!"

I look at her as if she's finally lost her mind.

"I thought it was dog poo…?" I go for the smile I reserve for the crazy people at work.

"No! Ha!" She's waving it around now and I hear something jangle. "That's already in the worm compost. These here are cans of Bud Light. Empties. Found them on my jog. Yep, the kids in the neighborhood must have had a fun time last Friday night!" she cackles.

"Well! Glad you're ah…on the case," I honestly don't know what else to say.

"You know what they say: JWAP! Jog With A Purpose!" She is shaking her head and waving at me as she closes her door.

I quickly give her a thumb's-up sign and wave, then hit the garage door button as if my life depended on it.

Dear God, I need some sleep.

Chapter Thirty

By the time we get to the weekend, I feel as if I am half-asleep and wired at the same time. This past week has been lived in a bubble and I don't even remember the last time James and I had a conversation resembling anything more than an exchange of information.

I've also eaten my fair share of Perfect Protein bars, proving our point. I'd rather eat food, but when you're on the go and buried in work…they're perfect.

"Now they just have to buy the premise," I wind up the story of my week at the same time we wind up dinner.

"They will. Think positive. When are you guys presenting?" James seems tired too.

"Monday." I lean back onto the sofa and let out air long held.

"Until then, what do we have on tap?" James swivels his head to look at me, and we both laugh from sheer exhaustion.

"Well, I would like to spend some time with Uncle Ben and Aunt Bunny this weekend. I know you saw them this week, but

I didn't, and I'm thinking a low-key dinner would be the perfect anecdote to the week we just had. Next weekend is Dez's shower, and the weekend after that is…the holidays." Which we still hadn't figured out, but I was in no mood to discuss right now.

"Okay, then let's head to bed. I'm beat, and I don't want to feel like a zombie all day tomorrow just because we felt compelled to stay up on a Friday night," James suggests as he lifts himself off the floor and reaches for the remote.

"I'm in!" I grab some of the detritus from dinner and do a speed-cleaning of the kitchen before padding off to bed.

I try to read but can barely keep my eyes open. By the time I go to click off my Kindle, James is softly snoring.

I don't remember turning on my side or actually drifting off to sleep. It seemed more like a thud, and when I wake up in the morning I am initially disoriented as to where I am and even who I am.

I roll over to find James still snoring next to me. The light is peeking through the windows and although I'm curious, I'm not ready to look at the clock yet. I want to stay in bed but my bladder is calling me, so I get up, take a quick pee, and check my phone. Once I'm convinced that the whole world hasn't blown up while we were sleeping, I put the phone down, stretch, yawn, and flip myself over to face James. After a few seconds of intently staring, his eyes flutter open and we share a silly grin.

"What time is it?" he inquires in a sleepy voice.

"Time for us?" I ask, hopeful, knowing that we desperately need some time to reconnect.

"Yes," he rolls over and hoists himself off the bed, making way for the bathroom. "Stay right there." He directs, then returns a few seconds later, making a big show of turning off his phone. We spend another glorious hour in bed and eventually decide it's time to get up.

The second he turns his phone back on, it rings, and I can tell by the tone of his voice that it's Vivian. He leaves the room and I languish a few minutes more, knowing that the minute my feet hit the floor, reality will also barrel its way through our bedroom.

As if on cue, James reenters the bedroom with a pained look on his face.

"My mother would like us to go to dinner with them tonight. They've already invited Uncle Ben and Aunt Bunny," he plops down next to me on the bed.

"Oh come on! I thought I had dibs on Uncle Ben and Aunt Bunny!" I say, careful to keep a playful tone in my voice. I can tell he's already annoyed, and I don't want to start the day off on the wrong proverbial foot.

"Apparently not when Vivian gets to them first," he sighs. "I just want a relaxing night, and whenever my mother's in charge it's…"

"Not relaxing?" I offer.

"Exactly." He pauses and then his whole face lights up. "How about I call her back, tell her we're busy, and take you out for a night on the town? Remember that piano bar we found downtown last Spring? We haven't been there since then! Let's go and tell Uncle Ben and Aunt Bunny that we'll stop by tomorrow and bring brunch. Thoughts?"

A part of me wants to go and indulge him and a part of me wants to be the good girl and fulfill our family obligations. I'm torn, so I pause a few seconds and do a quick evaluation of my life right now: all work and no play has made Rhonda a truly dull girl.

"Do you think we can get away with it?" I rub my hands together as if we're cooking up something.

"I will make sure of it," he assures me, and then picks up his cell to dial Vivian back. He puts on his best business voice and no matter how far away he roams, I can still hear her squawking through the phone. I giggle and burrow deeper into the covers.

After dealing with her, I hear his voice lift as he talks with who I presume is Uncle Ben. I've shut my eyes and allowed my body to relax, so by the time I see him again, I'm almost dozing off.

"We are all set for tomorrow," he informs me while climbing back in, "I told Uncle Ben we'd be there at eleven with bagels and lox."

"That sounds good," I smile in my state of near-sleep.

"And I'm setting an alarm for right now," he reaches over, grabs his phone once more, and then sets it back on the nightstand.

"That sounds even better," I curl into him, my wishes for the day having been granted, my body and soul content.

Chapter Thirty-One

"I can't remember the last time we went to bed at two in the morning," James drawls, his voice deep and husky, his eyes half closed.

"I can't remember the last time I drank that much wine," I respond, my voice also deeper, scratchy and raw.

"We need to do that more often," James suggests, hoisting his head in his hand and leaning on one elbow. "Rhonda, do you think if you wrote it in your calendar we could actually make it happen?"

"Oh, hardy-har-har," I roll my eyes but laugh because it's true.

He laughs himself and then rolls out of bed. "Come on, I still have to pick up the stuff for brunch."

I groan but follow him, eager to get my hands on a fresh bagel from our favorite place. About an hour later, we pull up to Aunt Bunny and Uncle Ben's laden with all the brunch items our hands can hold.

"Ah, I just made a fresh pot of coffee!" Uncle Ben exclaims as he pulls open the door and greets us. He grabs the brown paper bag full of warm bagels out of my hand and sticks his nose right in it. "These are the joys of life," he sniffs.

I wait until we've all got free hands and then I open my arms wide, waiting for Uncle Ben's signature hug. He doesn't disappoint.

"I've missed you," I tell him as he holds me close.

"I've missed you too," he stands back and then draws me in again. After we step apart, he indicates James. "I'm actually quite sick of seeing him!"

We laugh and then Aunt Bunny joins us from upstairs. She looks good but tired, and it's great to see her too.

"Ben, I chilled some champagne last night. Go make these kids some mimosas!" Aunt Bunny shoos him away with a smile.

"Ooohh, can I help?" I'm eager to talk to Uncle Ben and thrilled that I don't have to share him today.

"Of course! How about you grab the strawberries?" He indicates a bowl full of strawberries that have already been cut in half.

While we put the mimosas together I fill him in on everything that's been going on at work.

"The only problem is that we really don't have a tag line," I wind up with this, still thinking about it, still rolling different sentences around in my head.

"It'll come," he assures me, and although I know he's right, our presentation with Splash is tomorrow, and I'd really like to keep my job.

"Sure you don't have anything up your sleeve this time?" I prod him, forever thankful he caused my lightbulb moment for the last campaign.

"I've got nothing!" He insists and then smiles fully. "Really, right now...I feel like I've got everything."

I feel myself begin to tear up for there's never been a truer statement. By the time we join James and Aunt Bunny at the table, our conversation is lively and I find myself feeling blessed to be a part of this particular crew. When conversation turns to dinner the night before, I feel even more blessed to have missed it.

"Apparently, your mother wants to throw Jill a baby shower, but Jill doesn't want one. Vivian, of course, is outraged. Keep in mind that she's related to Ira. So Vivian has taken it upon herself to call Jill's mother and pressure her into a...what was she calling it, Bunny?" Uncle Ben asks her.

"A Ladies Tea," Aunt Bunny practically blanches. Vivian may be her sister, but they are not too much alike, as evidenced by the look of disdain on Aunt Bunny's face.

"Which is basically the same thing?" James is already shaking his head, even as he asks the question.

"Well..." I offer a hand gesture that means sort of.

"The thing is that Jill is afraid she's going to jinx it," Aunt Bunny offers this very matter-of-factly with an almost imperceptible shrug. "And I get it. I mean, I had several miscarriages, and this was back in the day, before IVF, before all that...and I know that I would have been very cautious as well. Vivian just doesn't get it. I mean, I love my sister...don't get me wrong. She just doesn't get...certain things."

"You are the Queen of Tact, Aunt Bunny," James toasts her with his mimosa and we all give in to a good laugh.

"When is she planning on kidnapping Jill for this event?" I'm curious as to how the whole thing will play out.

"She's aiming for next weekend. Jill's mother is reluctantly on board, but Ira's afraid of Jill, so he wants nothing to do with getting her there," Aunt Bunny sighs.

"Ira's a putz," Uncle Ben offers and I almost spit out my drink.

"To Ira!" James lifts his drink up high and clinks it with the one I just put down.

We all laugh and the next thing we know, we've moved on to talking about other things, and soon it's time to go.

"Good luck tomorrow," Uncle Ben says to me as he walks us out to our car. "You'll do fine."

"Thanks, Uncle Ben. I hope so."

Chapter Thirty-Two

"Are you ready?" Dez sticks her head into my office just as I close the lid on my laptop.

"As ready as I'll ever be," I reply as I grab my stuff. It's Monday, which means it's go-time.

"My only question is this: did we ever come up with a tag line?"

"I don't think so. We threw out a whole bunch of scenarios and never really decided on a one-liner that summed it all up. I think Artie was hoping to get away on concept and humor."

"Artie? Humor? Now, that's a concept," Dez comments as we walk into the conference room, each of us gearing up for whatever lies ahead. The room is full of all sorts of Team Splash people, and seconds after I pull out my chair, Artie struts in with an actual suit on.

"Artie! You look smashing!" Madeline, who is the head of the Art Department, is the only person I know that can get away with saying this to Artie. Perhaps it's the British accent.

He acknowledges her with air kisses and then snaps his fingers to get everyone's attention. "Okay, Team! They will be here momentarily. We have some great ideas, so let's be confident that they'll like what we've done so far. Anyone crush it and come up with a killer tag line over the weekend?"

Lots of tapping of pens and murmuring, but no one bolts up out of their seat wanting to take the credit. I exchange a look with Dez, motioning towards the water bottles. Apparently we're pulling out all stops today: Splash flavored water is carefully positioned throughout the room, and there are baskets of Perfect Protein bars strategically placed right by the entrance.

The buzzer sounds and we all fall silent.

"They're on their way," Helene from reception sing-songs into the speaker.

Artie stops pacing and strides towards the entrance, meeting the executives from Splash with a firm handshake and various pleasantries. Once the introductions are made, they take their seats and Dez and I begin to pitch our ideas: guy stuck in traffic/weary Mom/NBA Star. We dive right in and pull out all stops. They voice some concern over paying a recognizable NBA star tons of money to endorse their product, but they seem to like what they're hearing, and the vibe in the room is good.

"What about some sort of tag line?" One executive, Mark or Max asks suddenly, "Do you guys have anything like 'Recycle Your Life?'"

I bite my lip and look at Artie for help. He seems to be mulling something, and then Dez jumps in and says, "We thought about something simple that would follow through all the different ads." She pauses, and I know she's winging it, so I cross my fingers under the table. "What about this: Life's Not Perfect... Perfect Protein?" She embellishes with a sweeping arm, as if writing it in the sky.

They nod and murmur but there's no "Eureka!" moment, and I feel like the air has been sucked out of the room. A few minutes later they gather their things, make all the appropriate noises, and leave. We're left staring at each other and for once the whole crew is silent.

"Well, we'll know soon enough," Artie intones, his fidgeting at an all-time high.

Soon after we gather all our things, Dez and I find ourselves at our favorite coffee spot, each of us wishing we were drinking something stronger.

"I feel like we could have come up with something...I don't know...bolder," Dez says eventually.

"I think we did a great job." I shrug.

"I hope we still have our jobs," she says this and shrugs too, leaning back into her favorite comfy chair. "Well...either way, it's done. It is what it is."

"I never understood that saying."

"I get it; I just hate it."

"It feels like giving up."

"It sounds like exhaustion."

"If a saying could smell, I'd say it smells like defeat."

"It is what it is," Dez repeats, and we both laugh. There's nothing more to do and we know it.

Chapter Thirty-Three

By Thursday, the company as a whole seems completely off-kilter, anxiety is palpable everywhere you turn, and nobody's chatting by the water cooler or hurling the usual insults.

"They say a watched phone never rings," Dez says this as she walks into my office, and I can't help but smile at my dear friend. The energy level as we await our collective fate is nothing if not nerve-racking.

"I think that's Mom advice thrown out to teenage girls from another era," I counter, "and not exactly a piece of business wisdom."

"Either way, have you heard anything?"

I glance at my silent phone while refreshing my email.

"Nada."

"Coffee?"

"Of course."

Once we settle in I change the topic, forcing myself not to focus on whatever could be going down at work.

"So are you looking forward to Saturday?" I was beginning to get excited myself.

"I'm starting to," Dez gives me a look. "A part of me still can't believe I'm doing this."

"Marrying Jack?" I'm taken aback for half a second.

"No! Oh God, no…he's…" and the smile evolves, the same one she always wears when he's around. "He's the guy I would have painted, if I ever picked up a brush. You know what I mean?"

"I get you," I nod.

"Just: the whole thing! The parents-coming-into-town Friday night dinner, the getting up and getting dressed up for a Saturday afternoon bridal shower, in which case I will hand out actual party favors…it's sort of like, who am I, and what did I do with Dez?"

"Keep in mind that Dez is still running away and getting married."

"I prefer to refer to it as a destination wedding."

"Semantics."

"You're tough. Thank God I have you. Otherwise I might be doing something silly like baking cupcakes and wearing a corsage."

I ball up my napkin and aim right for her nose. It hits her chin and she glares at me.

"Should we go back?"

"We should."

We exit our coffee nirvana and trudge back to work, both of us taking our sweet time getting there. By the time I am sitting behind my desk, I decide once again to declutter, as the more organized I am, the more in control I feel.

It works for a bit, but my mind is flying in a hundred different directions: What if we don't pull this one off? Will the client–our biggest client–really pull all their business from our shop? Should I be floating a resume just in case? What if Dez loses her job right before her wedding? Did I ever follow up with the three people that never RSVP'ed for her shower? Are they coming or not? Why would you not RSVP for something? Was it an oversight, or some passive-aggressive garbage that I now need to deal with? I start a fight in my head with the one person who I know beyond a shadow of a doubt had always envied Dez (I swear I don't even know how she made the list) and just as I'm about to tell her off royally, my cell phone rings.

It's Vivian.

This is particularly interesting because Vivian almost never calls me directly. She either calls James on his cell, or sometimes buzzes us on the home phone. As I'm contemplating this, I pick up the phone and try to insert a smile in my voice.

"So! Are you all ready for Saturday?" Vivian uses this as her way of greeting me.

"Well, hello Vivian! Yes...I...I'm almost all set," I find it odd that she's interested in a shower she wasn't invited to, but far be it from me to guess her motivation.

"Well, it's always hectic right before an event, but it's always worth it in the end, isn't it?" Vivian proclaims this as if she is a fountain of wisdom.

I can hear her deep breath in, and I picture her taking a long drag off a cigarette. My nose instantly crinkles.

"It usually is," I agree, not exactly sure where she's headed. "Have you seen Aunt Bunny today?"

"I did. I saw her for coffee and I brought over an old-fashioned strudel, which she loved. The way I see it is that the ones who are reluctant to celebrate always seem to love the party the most, don't you agree?" she puffs.

"Totally," I agree, thinking of Dez, hoping she'll like the choices I made and the effort everyone is putting in to make her feel special. "Oh! Do you think we should have some sort of a celebration for Aunt Bunny? I know a woman at work who had a 'Kick Cancer's Ass' party. It was particularly funny because she had colon cancer, and she said–"

"How gauche," Vivian tsks. "I think we should wait until she's proclaimed remission status, and then I'll order platters."

"Oh. Of course," I can't quite think of anything else to say.

"We've got time," Vivian says, and I picture her blowing smoke rings in the brief pause, "I'll see you soon."

She abruptly hangs up the phone and I'm left wondering what the point of that conversation was. I think about texting James, realize he's in a meeting right now, and let it go. I've got so many other things on my current plate that the need to organize has never felt greater.

Chapter Thirty-Four

Friday was pretty much a repeat of Thursday at the agency; all of us on edge while pretending not to be. It was exhausting and by the time I got home Friday night, I was pleased as punch to see that James had taken the reigns and ordered Thai food for us to enjoy at home in comfy clothes.

"So what are your plans for tomorrow?" I ask as I shovel Pad Thai in my mouth at an alarming rate.

"Jack asked me if I wanted to join his family members who are not attending the shower in a friendly game of darts." James replies, his face also full.

"So you're going drinking with the guys?"

"Exactly."

"That sounds lovely, if typical," I sigh. I place my weary fork down finally, and lean back on the floor pillow that's propped behind my back.

"Are you looking forward to the shower?" James inquires as he sets his fork down as well.

"I am. I think that Dez will enjoy it, even though she isn't sure, and I know the people at the shelter will love being the recipients of cupcakes galore," I muse. "I'm just stressed out about work, and I still don't know what's going on for the holidays…which is next weekend already."

"Did you speak to my mother?"

"Yes. Did you know that she called me this week? Very strange. Anyway, she didn't say anything about the holidays… should I plan for both? Are you going to talk to Uncle Ben anytime soon? Do you think you can try and tactfully get an answer out of him?"

"I'll try. I told him I'd pop by tomorrow after darts," James shrugs. "Knowing you, you probably already have a lasagna or two hidden in the freezer."

"Those are backups."

"Exactly."

"And it's stuffed shells."

"Whatever."

"They are drastically different."

"Do you want to fight about this?"

"I'd rather get to bed early, and try and get some decent sleep before my best friend's bridal shower tomorrow."

"I'd rather get you to bed quite late," he whispers as he draws me close, and I fall into him, happy to be home.

Chapter Thirty-Five

Saturday morning arrives and the chaos kicks into high gear before I'm even out of the shower. I'm towel-drying my hair before I decide to finally turn off the notification bell on my phone–as every time it dings I find myself looking at the clock and getting anxious. My mind wanders, and I wonder how they managed to pull off showers back in the day. I can remember my mother telling me stories about all the white lies being told in order for her shower to be a big surprise.

It's hard enough to coordinate everyone without trying to keep it all a big fat secret from Dez. Dez and I don't have any secrets.

By the time I'm pulling on heels, Amalia is calling me to insist that Dez shouldn't be driving anyone to her own shower. I explain to her, once again, that Jack's family is from Maine, and that Dez offered to drive. Amalia is not convinced that this is a good idea, and in fact, continues to complain about various things until I insist I have to get going. I had offered to pick up

Jazz, and I don't want to be late, because I still want to set up some flowers and get all the party favors arranged in a basket before everyone else shows up.

The next hour is filled with grabbing Jazz, the flowers, getting to the venue, arranging everything the best way possible and greeting each guest as they file in. I meet Jack's Mom and I am genuinely happy for Dez as I take her in; she is the antithesis of all things Vivian. Soon we're baking cupcakes, and I feel as if the day is flying by. Even though I've barely had a chance to speak to Dez, I hear her laughing across the room, and I know that it's all good. We eat a fabulous brunch while the cupcakes are cooling, and by the time we're decorating, I look around and catch Amalia seeming to have a good time out of the corner of my eye.

Finally, I exhale.

It's not that I didn't think I'd pull it off; I always do, but there was something about this day that I hoped would be nothing less than perfect. Dez would argue that it's because of her choice to have a destination wedding that I've put so much emphasis on the shower, but it's actually only about the love I have for her, the fact that she knocked herself out for me when it was my turn to get married, and I simply want to return the favor.

By the end of the day, it's goodbyes and air kisses all around, with newfound friends looking forward to seeing each other again in St. Lucia. Amalia makes a comment about having to travel for the wedding, but Dez just ignores her, and I take her cue and do the same. Eventually, Dez, Jazz, Valentina and I pack up the cupcakes and take them over to the shelter. There my heart expands even more when I see the delight on the faces of the women receiving our cupcakes. They're happy for Dez and unfazed by our shoddy decorations; one particular character named Pia takes an entire box and proceeds to hoard them in her room. We laugh and share stories, and by the time I know it, the day is done, and it's beginning to get dark outside.

"Did you have a good time?" I ask Dez as I drape my arm around her. We walk over to our cars as I eagerly await her answer.

"I did," she nods and smiles, a genuine smile that she can't hide. "Thank you, my friend. You gave me a perfect day."

"Awww, that was the plan!" I give her a hug.

"You think the guys are back yet?" She looks at her watch.

"I have no idea," I pause. "You know how I know today was a great day?"

"How?" She tilts her head, humoring me.

"I haven't looked at my phone for hours."

"Me neither. I only hope somebody got pictures," she muses.

"I think your cousin Valentina already posted the entire shower on Instagram," I fill her in, and we laugh again, because it was one of those days we'll remember for a long, long time.

Chapter Thirty-Six

By the time I get home and kick off my heels, I realize I really do need to look at my phone, if for no other reason than to find out where James is, as the house is dark and I'm wondering if he already ate.

I pull my phone out of my purse and I'm instantly alarmed by the amount of missed calls I see; there's one from James, but it looks like thirty-seven from Vivian. Why on Earth would Vivian call me thirty-seven times? I hit James' number first and plead with God with each ring, praying he'll pick up the phone while my heart is hammering in my chest.

"Hey!" He sounds as if he's shouting, but there's so much background noise I can barely hear him.

"Hey! James! Where are you? Are you okay?" I'm shouting back at him, my mind already conjuring up a thousand different scenarios as to why Vivian was blowing up my phone.

"I'm great. I actually harassed Uncle Ben into coming with us, so I'm over here forcing the Wine Guy to have a beer while I get killed at darts," he laughs, and I realize he's talking to someone else while he's talking to me.

"James, do you have any idea why Vivian was calling me? I just walked in from Dez's shower and it seems like she's been calling me all day," I'm not sure what to think.

"Well, I don't know..." he pauses a second and it seems like he's talking to Uncle Ben. "Oh, it's probably about that tea thing she's doing for Jill. Who cares? Listen, I've got a plate of wings over here that's not going to eat itself. Why don't you come meet us? Jack's Dad is hilarious," he adds.

I look at my phone, the clock, and make a split decision. "I'll be there in a few." I jump into casual clothes, cool boots that are actually comfortable, and grab my phone as I run back out the door. Once I'm back in the car, I dial Dez.

"Dez, are you meeting the guys?" There seems to be a lot of noise over on her end as well.

"I wasn't planning to...why?" She says something to someone else. "Where are you?"

"I'm heading over to the sports bar they're at, and I was going to offer to pick you up too."

"Hold on a sec," I hear her asking someone something and a second later she's back on the line. "We'll meet you there."

"Cool!" I find myself blasting the radio on the way over to where the guys are, excited by the prospect of extending the day. The traffic is nonexistent, so about ten minutes after hanging up with Dez, I am sailing into the sports bar to find both James and Uncle Ben hanging out by a pool table, each with a full mug of beer in their hand. By the time Dez walks in with Amalia, her mother-in-law-to-be and Valentina, we decide to order another tray of wings and loaded potato skins for the crowd.

"Now, this is a perfect closeout to an amazing day!" Dez smashes her mug of beer into mine, and I agree wholeheartedly.

"I actually didn't think I could eat another thing, but…here I am," I say while hoisting a potato skin into my mouth.

"Do you know what the *second* question was that Jack asked me when he saw me?" She leans over and grabs a potato skin for herself.

"Wait, what was the first?"

"Well, the first thing he asked was about the shower, which is why I'm marrying him," Dez concedes with a smile.

"And so the second one was…?"

"Did we save him any cupcakes?"

"Of course! Did you?"

"Of course!" she grins. "I am marrying the guy." With that, she slides off the stool and traipses over to Jack, planting herself directly in front of him and demanding a kiss. Jack's Dad begins to hoot and holler and the next thing we know, we've ordered more beer and Uncle Ben starts dividing us up into teams for darts.

We play darts like the amateurs that we are, and we laugh, and drink, and practically close out the bar. Our impromptu night is so much fun that I completely forget to call back Vivian.

Chapter Thirty-Seven

"And where were you?!" Her voice bellows through the phone and it takes me a full minute to realize where I am, that I'm not in the middle of a nightmare, and that Vivian is in fact calling my cell phone once again.

"I'm sorry?" I mutter that or something equivalent but I can't seem to focus in because obviously someone is playing the drums somewhere inside my house. Or my head.

"Rhonda! Wake up! What happened to you yesterday?" Vivian barks, and I am reminded of Miranda Priestly, the awful boss in *The Devil Wears Prada*.

Except Vivian is inherently Prada-less.

"Yesterday?" I'm waking up, but it's all a bit fuzzy.

"Yesterday was Jill's Baby Tea!" she proclaims.

"Yesterday was also Dez's Wedding Shower," I return, finally waking up enough to slowly get heated. "You knew that, Vivian."

"And you knew that I expected you at Jill's Tea," she declares as if the Queen has spoken.

It suddenly dawns on me that *that* was why she called me the other day, and that she hadn't been talking about Dez at all, but about Jill. And that's also the reason why she rang my phone thirty-seven times yesterday.

I snap awake.

"Really, Vivian? How on Earth was I supposed to 'know' that?" I'm wrapping the word *know* in air quotes even though she can't see me. I sit up on the bed, and my rustling awakens James, who looks as if he's about to have an epic hangover.

"I called you the other day!" She's shrieking now.

"Sure, you called me the other day, but did you at any one point ask me if I would be attending Jill's shower? Or if I even could...? You know full well that I've been trying to get everything together for Dez's shower–"

"I did not throw Jill a shower; I threw her a tea," she clarifies as if it matters.

"Whatever," I dismiss her outright, and I'm about to tell her how I really feel when she decides to get down and dirty.

"Whatever? Of course, I should have known. If it doesn't matter to you, it simply doesn't matter. You've shown your true colors throughout the entire ordeal with our family and now you want to–"

"Want to what? And what exactly do you mean by true colors?" I'm fuming now, and James is holding his head beside me, but I can tell he's been listening to every word.

"Obviously our family has not been high on your priority list! You haven't been around! This last incident is the icing on the cake!" She's huffing into the phone.

"I actually have no idea what you're talking about. I've been dealing with a huge campaign at work, James and I have been incredibly busy, and you never invited me to the TEA that, by the way, Jill didn't WANT TO HAVE ANYWAY!" I don't realize I'm screaming until I stop and then process the fact that there is pure silence on the other end of the phone.

A second later, the line disconnects and I realize she hung up on me. Wishing for an old-school phone I can bang down, I hit the end button on my phone and fling it across the comforter.

"What," James hesitates, and his voice sounds like hell, "was that?"

"She hung up on me." I can't believe she did it, but at the same time I can. Vivian loves having the last word.

"I guess what I'm asking is: what the hell happened?" James clears his throat and attempts to sit up.

"I honestly don't know," I shake my head. "Did she say anything to you about expecting me to go to Jill's 'Tea' this weekend?"

"Not that I recall."

"And are you angry with me for any reason? For not being around, for...how did she put it? Not being supportive...I'm assuming she's referring to Aunt Bunny, but I have no real idea, since she's obviously not clear, and on top of that she expects that I'll read her mind!" I let out a sound that says nothing and everything and I fix my eyes on James.

"First of all," James says as he attempts to swing his legs to the side of the bed, "I need two Advil, and some water, and then perhaps I can make some sense of all this."

I sit up and adjust the pillows behind me while I wait for him to get what he needs and answer me. My mind keeps going over our conversation earlier this week. Was there ever a time she mentioned Jill specifically? And does she really feel like I've been blowing everybody off lately? I'm not so sure I care how she feels, but I do care how James feels, and by the time he heads back into the bedroom, I'm ready to get to the bottom of it.

"So? Are you able to talk to me now?" I'm about to launch into a full tirade.

"Barely," he toasts the air with a bottle of water. "I totally didn't think I drank that much yesterday, but...apparently I did," he groans. "Not quite sure if I should eat or shower."

"I don't know what to tell you." I want his sympathy and concern, but he doesn't appear quite up to the task, at least not yet.

"Listen," he looks at me directly, searching my face. "I'll deal with Vivian."

"It's not that. I dealt with her just now. I'm fully capable," I remind him. "It's just that she's being ridiculous. I mean, she's always ridiculous, but this time I feel like she's looking for someone to blame, and I'm not having it."

"Then don't," he says, sauntering slowly away from me. I hear the water turn on for the shower and eventually hear him get in. I sit there and fume for a little while longer and then decide to go out for a long walk. I shoot him a quick text and go while he's still in the shower. I've had enough of her, and I don't necessarily want to fight with him.

Chapter Thirty-Eight

What started out as a sweet and fun-filled weekend now felt sour and twisted. On my walk I checked in with myself and went over both conversations with Vivian, and by the time I hit my first hill I knew for certain that no matter how she couched it, she had never once clearly invited me to help, attend, or be a part of Jill's 'Tea.'

That said, I knew full well that what was really bothering me was all the other insinuations she made about how I was being selfish or uninvolved or whatever other else she threw out at me. I thought long and hard about what she said. The truth is that I had been incredibly preoccupied by my current work campaign, but I still felt that I was trying my damndest to juggle all the balls. I made time for Aunt Bunny when I could and sent food over when I couldn't; in fact, I was the one who kept continuously offering to host both Passover and Easter in the event that Aunt Bunny and Uncle Ben could not...and I still didn't even know what we were doing for either holiday! I had barely spent any time with my own husband lately; did she really expect me to drop everything and be there at her whim, fulfilling unspoken family obligations? I felt righteous anger flooding my body, and instead of walking it off, by the time I returned to our house, I felt sure I could strangle Vivian and not even feel remorse.

I stretched outside a bit before I went in, reminding myself that none of this was James' fault. For some reason, it was very tempting to lash out at him and make it his fault–after all, Vivian was his mother–but what I really wanted to do was talk and unwind, so I tried to focus on that.

"I'm home," I call out tentatively, not really sure where he was in the house, and equally unsure that he hadn't headed back to bed.

"I'm in the kitchen," he calls back, and I find him there, sitting at the island with a cup of coffee in front of him. "Want one?" He gestures to the steaming mug.

"Sure," I shrug. I down some water so that I can say I had the correct post-workout beverage, but it's Sunday morning and my body needs coffee.

"Feeling better?" We both say it at the same instant, and then we look at each other and laugh. One laugh leads to another and soon he pulls me close and starts kissing one cheek, then the other, all the while convincing me that he's almost back to normal.

"I daresay we were having such a good time that I didn't keep track of how much I was drinking, and I probably deserve this massive headache as well as anything else that comes my way," James says as he pours my coffee.

"I'm glad you had a good time. I did too, and it was fun

meeting you guys after. My only regret is that your mother had to go ahead and spoil it," I say this with a punch in my voice, and I realize that I'm at a point where I really can't help myself.

"Listen, I know you're upset with her and I don't blame you." He levels his gaze. "What would you like me to do?"

"I don't know. Can you think of a good place to hide the body?"

"That falls under the funny but not category, Rhonda," he warns.

"Not for you, maybe..." I sigh, letting the insinuation hang languidly in the air. "I simply can't do any more. I don't get her; I don't think I ever will, and I'm tired of everyone's expectations of me."

"Who's everyone?"

"Vivian, for starters," I let out a deep breath I didn't realize I had been holding. "And I can't really put my finger on the rest. I just feel like I'm supposed to come up with a career-saving campaign at work, throw the best bridal shower, host the holidays as if the Queen is coming to dinner, play nice in the sandbox with my father's twelve year-old girlfriend...you know, pay attention to you occasionally...find time for everyone...understand everything...I feel like I am supposed to be all things to all people and I just can't do it all!" I unexpectedly burst into tears.

"Well," James goes to reheat his coffee in the microwave. As the door swings shut he says, "From what I heard last night you did manage to throw the best bridal shower." He splays his hands.

"Great!" I mimic him. "Fabulous! I'm expecting an award any minute. You do understand what I'm getting at?" I'm so frustrated, and now I'm sniffling and snorting and I'm quite sure I look how I feel: a mess.

"I get it. I do. But here's the deal: you do this to yourself, Rhonda. Sure, Vivian is always going to try and push your buttons, but come on…you know you push yourself all the time, put in all the effort, and now you want to sit here and say that everyone else puts pressure on you?"

"You don't see it."

"I'm trying to."

"It's unspoken."

"Then it doesn't matter." He lifts the coffee back out of the microwave and takes a cautious sip. "Listen, are we okay?"

"Us?"

"Yes, the two of us." He looks around the room as if to find someone else standing there.

"I think so," I'm not sure where he's going, so I'm being cautious too.

"Isn't that all that matters? I mean, look, if you lose your job, that would suck, right? But we'd be okay. And if Vivian is pissy, so what? I'm okay with that being her almost constant state of being. Dez obviously loved her shower and the wedding is going to be great. Aunt Bunny seems like she's doing better every day. I get that it's a lot at once, but since when does life come at you in intervals? It is what it is."

"I hate that expression."

"I know that." He offers me a half-smile. "But sometimes it fits."

Chapter Thirty-Nine

The next thing I knew it was Wednesday. Hump Day. Two days before Passover, four before Easter, and all the phones in my world seemed to be on silent mode.

At work, Team Perfect Protein was in a tizzy because no one from Splash had gotten back to us. Artie was in and out of the office, trying hard to avoid the rest of the team, while the remainder of us were trying to keep busy until we heard something from him. Vivian had yet to call me back, and I was determined to not call her, if for no other reason than the fact that I felt that she was the one who needed to make amends this time around. I had left a message for Uncle Ben–figuring I would pick his brain about the holidays–but so far hadn't heard back.

I tried James at one point mid-morning and had that call go straight to voicemail as well.

"I give up!" I shouted to no one in particular. On that note, I stood up and grabbed my purse, launching myself over to Dez's office. I needed to stop with the phone for a while.

"Yes?" She was actually grinning as I strode into her office. The nerve!

I gestured towards the phone that was currently under her chin.

"It's Jack. He just booked us a romantic dinner on the beach," she filled me in, "but now I'm on hold."

"Story of my life!" I huffed as I sat down in the chair opposite her. "Coffee?" I mouthed the word to her as she began talking again. She nodded. A few minutes later, she hung up and we were off.

"Where is everyone?" Dez swung her arm around the empty reception area as we got on the elevator.

"Hiding?" I suggested.

"I'm trying not to focus on the radio silence, but..." she shrugged as we made our way outside.

"I'm determined not to," I agreed with her although my heart wasn't in it.

"I'm buying," Dez insisted and then practically forced me into our favorite set of chairs.

I was about to tell her what I wanted, but realized she knew. In the couple of minutes that it took her to grab our order, I sat as still as possible, feeling as if my head was about to explode.

"That bad, huh?" Dez slid me a very big coffee, waking me out of my reverie.

"I still don't know what we're doing for the holidays, and I refuse to call Vivian," I sounded like a petulant child even to my own ears.

"I can't say as I blame you," Dez sighed. "Do you want James to intervene?"

"Yes. No. I don't know," I pulled a face at the same moment that my phone pinged. "Ah! At least Uncle Ben is getting back to me!" I scanned his text quickly and thought to answer him later.

"What did he say?"

"Something about Aunt Bunny forcing him to go get his prostate checked. Can't say I blame her," I took a long sip of coffee and let the mocha flavor roll around on my tongue.

Liquid therapy at its best.

"So listen: since Jack's whole family was just here for the shower and Amalia is heading over to her new friend's house for Easter," Dez pauses as she rolls her eyes, so I assume the new friend is of the male persuasion, "how would you like to inherit us for Easter?"

"That's the best news I heard all day!"

"About Easter? I crash most of your Holidays," Dez reminds me.

"That and that little tidbit about Amalia. Who's the new friend?"

"Some guy she met at church?"

"And?"

"I don't have any details yet, and of course I refuse to get excited, because the other idiot is always lurking in the background, but you're right…it could possibly be very good news."

"You never know," I say this with enthusiasm.

"True," she acquiesces.

We sip and are both silent for a long moment, each of us lost in our own thoughts. I decide that this might be the mark of a true friendship; even more than knowing the way I take my coffee.

Eventually we leave and head back to a subdued office, all of us marking time until the head honchos decide exactly what they want. I do some upkeep that's called for with other accounts, then decide to attack the never-ending pile on my desk. By mid-afternoon I sit down and think about what I want to make for Easter, and just as I begin jotting things down on my list, I realize I never did text back Uncle Ben.

So how'd it go? I inquire with an emoticon that manages to look both shocked and appalled.

More fun than I can handle. He sends me back a laughing/crying emoticon.

I smile.

He's my unmitigated favorite in the family sweepstakes.

So what's up for Passover? I need to know.

We're having it here. We might pull a Vivian and order some things, but we want to keep with our tradition.

Yay! Please let me know what I can bring.

You. You and that guy you're married to.

A few more emoticons pass between us, and I eventually stop texting and lean back in my chair. I tap my pen and figure I've got two more days to figure out exactly what to do about Vivian. I think of my mother and I know what she would say. It kills me to think that my mother would tell me to kill her...with kindness.

Chapter Forty

"If I dip the apricots in dark chocolate, is that considered kosher?" I ask James this over my shoulder as I begin pulling melting chocolate from the cabinet.

"We're not kosher."

"You know what I mean." I roll my eyes. "I'm pretty sure your mother will be bringing macaroons, and I wanted to bring something else for dessert."

"Well, I love them…if that means anything." He stops, jumps up on the counter, and starts swinging his legs like a kid as he pilfers a dried apricot from the opened bag. "By the way…what exactly is the play with Vivian?"

"The play?" I'm not exactly sure what he's asking.

"I mean, are we going to walk in and be jovial, pretend as if nothing ever transpired between the two of you, or are we going to accost her in the driveway, getting it all out in the open before entry? Perhaps we can bypass both scenarios and just sprinkle some valium in her matzo ball soup?" he suggests with a glint in his eye.

"I haven't actually thought about the soup angle, but my gut feeling is that Vivian will react in her usual passive-aggressive manner, which basically means that she'll be jovial to everyone while shooting me the daggers," I offer with a shrug.

"So what do you suggest I do?"

"Nothing?"

"And you're going to be happy with that?"

"I'm quite all right," I insist, happy he's asked, but knowing that I can deal with Vivian. Ever since our discussion during that very first holiday season spent together as a family, I felt that we had come to some sort of understanding. I understand that she will always be a pain in the ass, and I think she understands that I'll play along, but when push comes to shove, that I will not be shoved.

Perhaps this Passover would present an opportunity to gently remind her of that fact.

"Okay then," James grabs a few more apricots in his fist before hopping off the counter.

"By the way, what time are we expected?"

"What time is sunset?" James pulls out his phone as I begin melting the chocolate.

"Should I get out early?" I surmise that this won't be a big deal since we've all been sitting around on our hands lately anyway.

"I will be," James answers me off-handedly, and by the time he's left the room I realize I didn't get a direct answer. I busy myself with the apricots, and then line them up like soldiers on wax paper so that they can dry themselves nicely in the fridge. By the time I tumble into bed, I find myself tired enough to read only a few pages before putting down my book.

The next morning is chaotic: James is rushing around to get to work early so he can get home early as well. I make it to work about the same time as always, happy to find a sign on an easel at reception reminding us that the office will be closed at noon.

"This is great. Both holidays falling this weekend means that no one can get their panties in a bunch," Ramon snarks as he points to the sign, directly before hopping on the elevator going down.

I shake my head and grin at the characters I spend my day with as I make my way down the hall in search of Dez.

"Happy Easter, Happy Spring: Happy, Happy Everything!" I singsong as I throw open her door and plop down on her squishy chair.

"Isn't it a bit early for you?"

"Well, we're only here until noon."

"True. So you should probably get it all out now."

"Any chance you want to crash the party tonight too?"

"Ha! Although I'd love to run interference for you a la Vivian, I have plans for dinner and I am volunteering early tomorrow at the shelter." She pauses. "By the way, what would you like me to bring on Sunday?"

"You. And that guy you're about to be married to," I borrow from Uncle Ben.

Chapter Forty-One

As fate would have it, James gets out later than expected, and by the time we both get home, change, grab the apricots and a bottle of wine, we just about make it over to Aunt Bunny and Uncle Ben's on time. Hence there is no altercation or reparation in the driveway, and my first glimpse of Vivian is her holding court at one end of the table, foisting her opinion of some such thing on Cousin David and Diana. They look as if they are being held against their will, or perhaps that's just my hot take. As we enter and greet everyone, Vivian cuts her eyes at me for a brief moment and offers me a smile that looks somewhat like a snarl. There's a lot of conversation going on around us, but she doesn't utter a word. James leans in to give her a kiss on the cheek and she allows it, acting as if the Queen is holding court, and I find myself trying hard not to chuckle at her lack of originality. I decide I will suffer through the night taking cues from whatever play she's decided to offer. I have no intention of being the bigger person, and although I can feel my mother's wisdom coursing through my veins, I ignore the inner voice that always wishes to do the right thing. Instead I offer that pesky nudge a full glass of wine, and take the seat farthest away from Vivian.

By the time Uncle Ben decides to ask The Four Questions, I am two very full glasses in.

"Why is this night different from all other nights?" Uncle Ben asks, and I stifle a sound. It's not; Vivian is acting as if the world has wronged her personally, which seems to be her constant demeanor.

We complete the ritual and then everyone begins to dig in; James has a pretty non-traditional family, so I assume we're done with the questions, and by the time the dinner is over, I'm already well into another glass of wine. When we're about to serve dessert, I decide that I'll be the bigger person and go over and give Vivian a hug.

"Just think, Jill: by this time next year, we'll have a child to open the door for Elijah!" Vivian is referring to the part of the tradition where a child is supposed to open the door for the Prophet Elijah to enter.

"I can't wait," Jill is rubbing her belly and beaming at the mere thought of what our next Passover will look like.

"I bet," I feel all warm and fuzzy and decide to give Jill a hug too. Just as I'm about to get up from the table, I feel Vivian shoot me the daggers. I push back from the table and offer her a huge smile.

Why not?

"I would've *bet* that Jill would have loved to have seen you on Saturday too," Vivian offers this out with a saccharine smile.

"Oh, Jill!" I turn towards her, my back to Vivian, the instant she decides to throw the first stone. "I'm so sorry Vivian didn't tell you about my best friend's bridal shower I was hosting." Two can play this game.

"It's okay," Jill waves me off, as she's starting to look a bit uncomfortable.

"Jill, you don't have to pretend that she didn't hurt your feelings," Vivian insists.

Then she actually picked up her drink and toasted me with a wink.

I look to Uncle Ben, but he's deep in conversation with James, and I feel as if I'm in the Twilight Zone. The nerve of this woman; the sheer gall! I wait a beat and then go for it.

"Jill, I'm actually sorry that Vivian didn't take *your* feelings into account when you said you weren't interested in the tea." I stare directly at Vivian and am tempted to throw down the proverbial mic.

Vivian snorts–loudly–and then scrapes back her chair. I see her screwing up her mouth, about to throw the next glancing blow when Diana saves the day.

"Ladies! Did you know that in my family, nobody ever has a shower, or a tea...or anything before the baby is born? Instead we have a gathering about a month after, where everyone brings the new Mom a covered dish, some baby things, and then passes around a calendar." Diana offers this out as if we've all won a great prize.

"Really?" Vivian scoffs.

"Absolutely," Diana nods vigorously.

"What's the calendar for?" I'm curious now.

"It's a way for each woman to offer to take the baby off the new Mom's hands. We give her the gift of some time, whether it be a date night, or a nap in the afternoon. I've heard that it's the best gift of all."

In an instant, I see how Diana is probably amazing at the job she does, getting people to surrender dogs in a way that makes them feel empowered. I tip my proverbial hat to her and decide to make my own mother proud.

"Jill," I say this loud and clear, "I'd love to be the first one to pick a date." I hear another snort-like sound from Vivian's side of the ring, but I choose to ignore her, pull my shoulders back, and head to the bathroom. I don't like her, and...far worse...I don't like the person I become when I'm around her.

I hustle into the bathroom and pull myself together. I need to shift my focus. No more wine, and no more petty barbs being thrown across a holiday table. I fix my hair and straighten my shirt. I nod to myself in the mirror and exit the room to find Diana waiting outside the bathroom door.

"Oh! Sorry, Diana...were you waiting long?" I'm fully aware that I'm a bit tipsy but have no real idea how long I was in the bathroom.

"No, you're good," she smiles. "Wait here a second."

She dips into the bathroom and I lean against the wall. I recognize that I probably shouldn't have had that last glass of wine, but I also know that I wasn't interested in sparring with Vivian without some liquid courage. I sigh, and wonder if and when it'll ever get any easier with her. I think about having a child–actually giving her a grandchild–and I shudder.

Just then, Diana exits the bathroom and links my arm in hers, pulling me towards the screened-in porch. It's an early spring night, warm, with a brisk undertone, winter still trying to hold its ground.

"Listen, girlfriend, I have no idea what her issue is, but…can I give you some unsolicited advice?" Diana stares at me in the semi-darkness.

"Yeah," I hesitate. I'm almost put off by her boldness, but I like Diana, and I know that in order to be an effective female police officer she's probably got to be bold every single day.

"Don't engage her."

"I wasn't trying to…"

"You may not have been, but you played into her hands and it's not good for you or your marriage. Look, I know I might be talking out of turn here; I just met you guys, and it's probably not my place to say a damn thing, but…she reminds me of one of my rescues."

"How so?"

"Well, she's scared shitless, but she's obviously all bark and no bite. For whatever reason, she's decided to egg you on, and you took the bait."

"Well, we had a misunderstanding…"

"Let it go. Jill knows what she's all about."

I give her a look that says I'm not so sure.

"Look, I've only met her twice before and I've got her number. Let her huff and puff and blow her own house down. Don't you help her to do it," Diana warns, her penetrating gaze locked on me.

"Tell me how you know all this," I shake my head. I didn't exactly underestimate her, but I think I figured that in order for her to be with David, well…I don't know what I thought.

"First, I've been married before," she begins. She waves that sentence away before it even has a moment to take hold. "Irrelevant. Starter marriage. Horrible in-laws. I was young and dumb. My ex-mother-in-law makes Vivian look like an amateur. My point is, I deal with women like her every day: the passive-aggressive middle-aged meddlesome mother who feels as if her opinion is all that matters. I'm telling you, she's scared, and it shows. Let her be. You don't need to duke it out with her here, now, or any time in the future. Just be you. You know that saying that everyone says now? You do you. That's my advice, unsolicited as it may be." She folds her arms across her chest and holds my gaze.

"You're probably right," I concede and blow out a deep breath, and it's still cold enough to see my breath hit the air. "I just hate how I feel about her, and worse yet, how I feel about myself when I'm around her."

"Well, you can change that." She looks over her shoulder and then gestures towards the dining room. "I charge big bucks for that kind of advice though," she laughs.

I laugh with her, thankful for her words of wisdom. "We have to exchange numbers before you leave," I insist.

"I'll call you right now." She whips her phone out of a pocket, and I give her my phone number. I don't have my phone on me, but I'll check it before I leave.

"Thanks," I say to her as we head back inside. I hear laughter and I smile as we rejoin the group. There's a platter full of maca-roons on the table now, so I reach out and help myself to one that's half-dipped in chocolate.

It's sweet and satisfying, crisp and chewy, and as I indulge in a second one, I taste the metaphor rolling around on my tongue. I find myself chuckling, and the next thing I know, the night is over and everyone is saying their goodbyes.

"I'll call you," Diana says as she gives me a full-on hug.

"Definitely," I hug her back and feel as if I've found a friend.

Chapter Forty-Two

"Did you ever notice there's no Easter music?" I mention as I cut up all the accoutrements for my make-your-own-omelette bar.

"What are you talking about? We just sang seventeen choruses of *What a Mighty God We Serve*," James points out with flourish.

"Ha! That's not what I mean and you know it. I mean, there's Christmas music, right? Tons of it, and technically Easter is the more significant day on the Christian calendar," I muse.

"Oh no...oh no you don't!" James is helping me slice grape tomatoes in half, but he stops cold and looks at me as if what I've suggested is heresy. "We've been down this road before. Remember the infamous rant about the Hanukkah music that doesn't exist? I can clearly recall Neil Diamond blocking you on Twitter for slamming the mere idea of him putting out a Christmas album."

"I understand his point about doing it for the fans, but..."

"But nothing! You get no Easter music and you like it!" He is shaking a knife at me as I slowly step away from him to begin another task.

"I'll put on jazz," I decide this is a happy medium.

"Great idea!" he shakes his head as I begin to filter in something that represents brunch, if not Easter.

We're almost done prepping, and I find myself eagerly awaiting Dez and Jack, hoping they arrive before anyone else. I'm in desperate need of buffer people today, determined to not let things go off the rails once again with Vivian. I even went so far as to text Diana last night and invite her and David at the last minute, hoping they would come fill the room, but David's working and Diana has her own family to visit.

I'm still happy we've connected though, and I intend to invite her out for a Ladies Night with Dez and I, plus whoever else is up for a good time after Dez's wedding.

I get my wish a few minutes later when James escorts Dez and Jack in, Dez sporting something that resembles an actual Easter bonnet.

"What's with the hat?" It's incredibly Dez and so unlike her at the same time.

"I'm being festive!" She gives me a look, and I hand her a mimosa.

"You are funniest person I know," I tell her and it's true. She doesn't even try; she simply is.

"And you're the most neurotic," she gives me a sly smile. "Wait! Did you actually color Easter eggs?" She points to the bright array of various colored eggs that are situated in a basket on my kitchen island.

"I did!" I'm proud like a five year old.

"I have no idea why we're friends," she teases.

"You'll love them," I insist. Just then, the doorbell rings, and I hear James and Jack saying hello to my Dad and Julia. I swipe at the counter and grab my mimosa, armed and ready for the next wave of guests.

They're followed soon after by Uncle Ben and Aunt Bunny, with Vivian and Vlad bringing up the rear. Once James makes sure everyone has a drink in their hand, I open up the omelette bar and encourage everyone to fill their plates from the stuff we have on the island, while I custom-make perfect half-moons and slide them one by one onto everyone's plate. I decided to do the brunch as casual as possible, with the idea in mind that people can fill their plates and linger here and there, no formal seating assigned.

Vivian seems to be avoiding me again–no omelette order for her–as she's busy talking to her son, so I determine to take Diana's advice today and let things be.

"Julia, can I fill your glass?" I indicate her empty champagne glass and as she nods, I begin shaking the orange juice.

"Thanks," she says, as I fill her up. "Rhonda, this is really wonderful. I've always wanted to do brunch on Easter, but my family usually does dinner." This sentence leads us to talking about family, and I find out through the course of the conversation that Dad is heading over to her sister's house later on for said dinner.

I take it they're getting serious.

"So are you all set for St. Lucia?" Uncle Ben and I are standing by the island, taking turns with the cream cheese and lox, and I smile as he piles his plate high for a second time.

"I think so," I nod, my mind still making internal lists of all the things that have to happen before we leave, and I allow myself to think briefly of work. My wish is that we'll know about the Perfect Protein campaign sooner rather than later; in my head I had envisioned going to Dez's wedding and our subsequent vacation with a proverbial clean plate.

"Aunt Bunny and I went there years ago on a cruise ship," Uncle Ben tells me between bites about the worst possible neighbors in the cabin next to them, and I laugh so hard at one point I almost choke.

Soon we're all trading traveling war stories and eventually the entire group is laughing. Even Vivian seems to be cracking a smile here and there.

The afternoon fades to early evening, and one by one, people begin to say their goodbyes.

"I have no idea how I'm going to eat again, but I'm willing to try," my father pats his nonexistent stomach and I catch a rather intimate smile pass between him and Julia.

"Well, good luck!" I announce to both of them.

Once Vivian and Vlad decide to leave, I give Vlad a hug and thank them both for coming. There's a certain energy that surrounds Vivian that warns me she's not up for a hug just yet. I wave to them from the door, then turn to find Uncle Ben and Aunt Bunny wishing Dez and Jack well.

"It's going to be perfect," Uncle Ben reassures Dez, "I can't wait to see all the pictures when you return."

"Thanks Uncle Ben," Dez hugs him and then Aunt Bunny. "We wish you could be there."

"We'll be there in spirit," Uncle Ben assures her and I find myself getting choked up as I take in the exchange. There's raw emotion bubbling right under the surface, and as I seek Aunt

Bunny's face, I realize how lucky we are to have them.

"I'll see you tomorrow," Dez squeezes me.

"Yes. Let's hope we can get this whole thing all wrapped up." She knows I'm talking about work, and we share a look as I knock on the wooden front hall table.

Dez and Jack are backing up out of our driveway when I realize I forgot something. I run into the kitchen and grab the plastic container I filled with hard-boiled eggs.

"Wait!" I call out to them and then run out the front door before they pull away. I run up to Dez's window and thrust the eggs at her, trying hard not to laugh.

"You're ridiculous!" She laughs at me but she still reaches her hand through the window and takes what I'm offering.

"I know!" I grin wickedly, "I can't help it."

Chapter Forty-Three

The second my foot steps off the elevator, I feel the energy in the ad agency has shifted, and I know something's up.

"What's going on?" I ask Helene, but she's on a call and holds up one finger.

I hustle into Dez's office, only to find her standing there commiserating with Ramon and Madeline.

"What's going on?" I demand for a second time in two minutes.

"WE GOT IT!" Dez yells and does a little dance and it takes me less than a nanosecond to join in and begin dancing around with her. I believe I throw my purse, and then we clasp hands and giggle like schoolgirls.

"Please tell me you mean Perfect Protein!" I yell at her, suddenly realizing that if she means something else we're screwed.

"What the hell else did you think I meant?" She laughs and Madeline and Ramon join in.

"Oh!" I throw myself on my favorite chair. "I feel like I can exhale!" I'm starting to feel as if I could cry as well, so I pop back up, and instead confront them with, "Does this mean we have a meeting?"

"That," Ramon says, "and a deadline. I'll see you guys in a bit." He lopes off after his pronouncement and we all start talking over each other. Once we figure out what's going on, we promise to meet up in the conference room in an hour and then go our separate ways. I'm floating as I enter my office, slam the door, toss my bag again and call James on speaker.

"Guess what?!" I'm so glad he picked up. I can barely contain myself.

"You guys got the account!" He guesses correctly.

"YES!" I'm overly excited at this point, and it occurs to me that I was quite possibly a bit more worried than I had allowed myself to feel the entire time we were hanging in the balance.

"Oh, babe...I'm so happy for you, so proud..." James is saying a myriad of things at this point, but I can barely hear him, as I allow myself to finally let go and cry. "Are you crying?"

"I am," I admit, although my throat is closed and I can barely shove out words. "Let me call you back."

I don't wait for him to answer, I simply hang up the phone and let it all hang out. I cry tears of joy, sniffling, snorting, somehow still surprised that I'm getting so emotional.

I didn't realize I was holding on so tightly. I just knew that I was afraid of losing my grip. The thought of them not giving us this account, and in fact yanking the other account I've spent countless hours working on and cultivating...the mere idea of the ad agency having to restructure...the ache I felt every time

I thought I'd lose my job...it's all bubbling over now in the form of big fat tears. Although I've known since I was a little girl that I hated anything I couldn't control, that feeling has only intensified since my mother died, and the past few months have been pockmarked with fear, the overarching theme being Things I Cannot Control. Aunt Bunny's illness, losing my job, my concern over Dez's wedding; even thoughts about my own marriage and family situation kept sneaking in and causing me to have a constant level of anxiety. It's been low-level and well hidden, but now it's forcing its way through my tear ducts, and I find myself breathing heavy, finally allowing myself to concentrate on my breathing, in and out, one breath at a time. Eventually, I get up and grab a fistful of tissues, happy for the privacy of a closed door. When I take a look in the mirror, I find my cheeks splotchy and my makeup all over the place. I make a face at my image, and then proceed to look myself over more carefully. What exactly is it that I'm feeling right now? Is it the sweet release of pent-up emotion, or is it a whole host of things that have been jammed up inside my heart? Today feels surreptitiously like a beginning and an ending all wrapped up into one.

I take another deep breath and try shaking it off. I need to reapply my makeup and join the others in the conference room in a short while. I give myself a mini pep talk and know that I can handle the next step.

All of them.

Chapter Forty-Four

The conference room is chaos, and after several congratulatory moments, Artie shushes all of us and we begin to come up with a plan and a timeline for Perfect Protein. It escapes no one's attention that both Dez and I will be gone for a week, (her for a bit more) but I determine that it will not stop either one of us from doing what we do best.

In the end, they decided that Life's Not Perfect: Perfect Protein was everything. We somehow convinced them that less is more; and they liked most of the scenarios we presented, although they did come back with a request for a couple of more. Just in case.

"Is it budget?" I ask, already doodling and jotting down a few key words that spring to mind as we talk.

"Meh," Artie splays his hands, "I'm not sure yet."

"Depends on what we come up with," Dez nods. "They'll be willing to spend if they love it."

"Exactly," I agree. We work on a few more odds and ends before Artie gives us the go-ahead to create. As we're leaving the conference room, Dez shoots me a worried look.

"Believe me when I say I'm thrilled that they went for it," she starts as I follow her into her office, " and of course thrilled that our jobs are secure…at least, for now. But can I also say that I'm absolutely paranoid that we're not going to hit any of our goals before I leave?"

"I get it," I was thinking the same thing. "But we can't focus on that. At this point, what else do you have to get done for the wedding?"

"The good news is…not much," she acquiesces. "The resort is supposed to be taking care of all the details. However, I still need to coordinate some things with them, and pack, and of course there's always last-minute stuff you have to shop for…" she trails off and I can see the gears turning, a mile a minute.

"I propose an online shopping festival of sorts…let's get as much work done as we can today, and then you go home and make a long list of everything you have left to shop for…I'll make one too, that way when we get coffee tomorrow, we'll go over said list, then nail it together tomorrow night." I'm pretty sure I have at least one more tray of stuffed shells in the freezer. That and a bottle of wine and we might be able to get a whole lot done.

"Sounds like a plan," Dez smiles. "Now let's get to work."

Chapter Forty-Five

The next few days rush by in an adrenaline-fueled blur: we work hard on the campaign, drink copious amounts of caffeine, make lists for the wedding, get together to online shop, eat, drink, and basically cross things off our lists together one by one.

By Friday, I'm wiped out. I arrive at home to a near mountain of boxes in the hallway, all from different websites, all of them needing my attention. I pass them by to find James softly snoring on the couch.

It's 8:30 pm.

"Hey there sweetie," I place my bag on the floor near him and kneel down so that we're face to face.

"Hey," his eyes flutter awake, and he smiles. "Looks like I dozed off for a bit. What time is it?"

I tell him, kiss him, and then encourage him to grab a bite to eat with me before he goes to sleep for the night.

"I got stuff," he informs me as he slides off the couch and directly onto a floor pillow.

"Stuff?" I laugh at him, but I know I'm not much more capable of stringing words together at this point. My brain is fried, and I'm just starting to hit a wall. I open the fridge to find classic Chinese food containers and I smile. "This looks like pretty good stuff."

"Glad you like it," James gets up to help and within a few minutes we're chomping.

"So how was your day?" I ask between bites.

"Do you mean my week?" He smirks.

"Exactly." I smile, thinking about how busy we've been and how much I'm starting to look forward to our upcoming vacation. I feel like we haven't had a real conversation in years, and I can't recall the last time I felt relaxed.

"It was fast. I can't believe it's Friday already and we're leaving next week," he yawns, then points to the front hall. "Is it safe to assume that next month's credit card bill is going to be a doozy?"

"Safe," I nod. "Thank God I have my job."

"Well, Amen to that!" He tosses his chopsticks on top of his plate. "Do you think Dez is starting to get nervous?"

"No," I muse, pulling apart a fortune cookie, "I think she's ready. If we can get a lot done this week, she can feel comfortable with that aspect, and then it's off to marry the love of her life. I think she's getting excited."

"I know I'm excited to have a pinà colada in my hand," James kisses me on the neck as he gets up to turn off the television.

"Ummm...me too." I can practically taste it.

Chapter Forty-Six

"Did you buy enough sunblock?" Dez looks at me as if I am a crazed lunatic, which I realize I may be, as I unpack a case full of various SPF potions.

"Well, they had some sort of a two-for-something deal, and then I figured that we'd all need some, so I ordered enough for everyone just in case someone forgot," I defend myself in the face of both lotion and spray.

"You do know they have a sundry store at the resort," Dez reminds me.

"That's great if you want to pay ninety-two dollars for an SPF 30 in a 6-ounce spray," I challenge her as I divvy it all up. "I like to be prepared."

"And that...is why I love you!" James chuckles as he passes us in the hallway.

I think I see he and Dez exchange a look but I don't catch it in time to really give them the jazz. Besides, we have enough to do. There's about 47 hours and counting until we leave, and I'm only about halfway packed. I refer to my list.

"Do you need me to pack or carry anything for you?" I offer, as I continue to manage my space in my head.

"I don't think so," Dez replies. "I've decided to carry-on the dress. I don't trust the airline to not lose my luggage, so I'm packing everything else, figuring," she shoots me a look, "if they lose my sunblock, I can always buy more."

"Oh, you're hilarious," I can't help but laugh at myself nonetheless.

"Ladies! Takeout is served!" James calls from the kitchen and after a few minutes we head in to eat with him and Jack.

"James, are you packed yet?" I have my suitcases out and open on the floor in our bedroom but I've yet to see his.

"Rhonda, can you trust that I will be packed by the time we're ready for takeoff?" James asks.

"No," I reply.

All three of them laugh at me.

"How are you not more stressed out?" I am in awe of Dez at this point.

"Because I refuse to be," she states plainly, and I know she's right. Her outlook is a large part of the reason she wanted to have a destination wedding to begin with. I hate to admit it, but I'm beginning to see the wisdom in her choice.

"And although anything can happen: a hurricane, family drama, a shark bite..." Jack trails off here with a wicked smile, "I'm really glad we decided to go this route. It feels right for us."

Dez's phone rings then and I see her make a face and give us the one-sec signal as she steps away from our takeout feast. A beat later I hear her giving the person on the other end terse one-word answers, and I wonder for a millisecond if it's another issue at work, but then I hear her burst into Spanish, her voice growing louder with each sentence, and I look to Jack.

"What the...?" I'm assuming it's Amalia, but it could be her cousin Valentina or any other family member.

Or Ramon...?

"I don't know," he shrugs, chews, puts down his fork. For a full minute, we're all eavesdropping on Dez, listening in to a stream of agitated Spanish. By the time she disconnects and walks back into the room, I'm more worried than curious.

"Spoke too soon." She shoots Jack an admonishing look.

"What just happened?" He gestures to the phone, and although he goes to move towards her, she moves away and begins pacing the room at lightning speed.

"That was Amalia," Dez huffs, "and she just wanted to let me know that Pedro is currently out of rehab, and would like nothing more than to escort her to our wedding."

By blood runs cold because I know that this was always Dez's worst-case-scenario/nightmare. I'm fully aware of how much she hates Pedro, and I assume Jack knows this too. We exchange a look.

"Whatever happened to the nice guy she met at church?" I'm pretty stunned by this latest turn of events, but my mind is reeling, and I blurt this out, as if it matters.

"Who knows? Who cares?" Dez gestures wildly with her hands. "All I know is that if she comes–if she shows up with this total piece of garbage–IF SHE THINKS SHE'S COMING TO MY WEDDING WITH THAT BASTARD ON HER ARM, I swear to God, I'll...OH! I'm calling Valentina right now and telling her that Omar may have to act as a bouncer!" Dez picks up her phone again and hits Valentina's number. She continues pacing and breathing fire through her nose.

"I thought Omar was a magician?" Jack says this sotto voce, directing the question to me as Dez begins wearing a hole in my floor.

"He is, but sometimes he bounces at the Magic Hat to make some extra money," I make a face to indicate that this fact is irrelevant.

"Valentina," Dez says, and then switches over quickly to Spanish.

I feel helpless and unsure of what to do next. James begins pouring more wine and quietly offers to reheat my dish.

I shoo him away.

By the time Dez hangs up the second time, there are tearstains on her cheeks. Her hand is visibly shaking as she reaches for her glass and gulps down the rest of her drink.

"What can I do? Do you want me to talk to Amalia?" I offer. "I can...I can call her, maybe explain to her that this is just not a good–"

"A good what? A good idea? A good time? Maybe if you explain it to her, you know, that her timing just sort of SUCKS, maybe that would help!" Dez snaps, practically spitting.

"If you want me to, I'll–"

Again, she cuts me off, ranting and raving about her mother and this fool Pedro who obviously everyone can see is a fool... everyone, of course, except Amalia.

I let her go to it, unsure of what I can offer to do to help. I'm about to take a breath and try again to get a word in edgewise, when Dez stops suddenly and simply shakes her head. Her shoulders sag and that's when I begin to feel frantic.

"Dez? Look, I can…" I begin to speak, but I'm not sure exactly what it is I should say, or even what I'm trying to do here.

She holds her hand up, full stop, and doesn't say a word.

Then she says in a strangled voice, "Rhonda, you can't fix this for me. Nobody can."

I reach for her, figuring a big hug might be just what she needs, but she shrugs me off and walks away. A second later, I hear my front door slam.

"I'm sorry," Jack practically whispers, his face a myriad of emotions. He runs after her and I hear the door close again.

I look to James and I'm about to say something, but for some reason, I'm the one bursting into tears.

Chapter Forty-Seven

"Should I call her? Text?" I've already waited Dez out a couple of hours; now that I'm through with breakfast and my preliminary packing, I find myself wringing my hands, unsure of how to approach the latest wedding development.

"I think if she needs you, she'll call you," James is trying like hell to reassure me, but I'm not convinced.

"I just feel like she must need me," I insist, my mind full of all the things I can think to do to help her through this unfair plot twist. I simultaneously find myself angry with Amalia; why on Earth would she spring this on her daughter at the last possible minute? And how could she even manage to do it? Was Pedro going to offer to buy himself a standby ticket, or was she thinking about jamming him in her suitcase, and then springing him on all of us as Dez and Jack take the floor for their first dance? Deep down, I know it's none of my business, but I can't help myself and I feel tempted to call Amalia and tell her how I really feel. I'd like to inform her that the entire reason Dez and Jack even decided to have a destination wedding was based on Dez not wanting to deal with the all too real possibility of Amalia foisting her paramour on Dez, and the event itself.

I sigh, loud as anything, and go grab my untouched coffee. I'm deciding whether to do a quick reheat in the microwave or brew another cup when I hear the doorbell ring.

I leave my mug and bound towards the door, convinced that it's Dez. I throw open the door to find my regular UPS guy instead, smiling his usual smile.

"Hey, Jay," I feel a bit embarrassed by the way I ripped open the door, but I'll get over it.

"Hey Rhonda," he nods as he hands me a small box of aloe vera gel.

"Thanks," I nod and wave, happy to see that the after-sun product that was on backorder made it on time. I head back to my coffee dilemma, and just as I go to toss the old cup, the doorbell rings again.

"I got it," I call to James, convinced that it's Jay and that I probably forgot to sign something.

It's Dez.

"Hey," she says awkwardly. She's got a baseball hat on backwards and she offers me a lopsided grin.

"Hey!" I swing the door open and usher her in. "You okay?"

"I'm..." she pauses in the doorway and looks as if she might cry for a moment. Then I see her draw a deep breath and step across the threshold. "I'm sorry."

"No, I'm sorry," I extend my arms out as an invitation.

A moment later we're hugging, and I hear the still, small voice inside that guides me to listen.

"So…" she exhales big here, and I follow her into my living room, waiting for her to unburden herself. "The whole thing with Amalia is beyond ridiculous."

She scoffs, pulls a throw pillow from my pile, and situates it on her lap before she proceeds. "Basically, this idiot Pedro seems to have some sort of a hold on her; I don't understand it and I never will. My mother who believes in almost nothing… she actually believes him every time he says he's healed, or he's changed, or whatever load of bull he tries to sell her. And I've gotten to the point where if she wants to buy it: fine. She can buy it. I don't have to anymore. I can't stand him. He knows how I feel and if ever I'm around when he is, he avoids me like the plague. I think he hates the fact that I can see right through him, and I don't even try to pretend anymore. I can't stand spending holidays with them; that's why so often I'm either volunteering at the shelter or hanging out with you. He ruins every good thing, including whatever relationship I had or have with my mother."

I take a throw pillow too and start playing with the tassels. I want Dez to get it all out and I'm determined not to interrupt her.

"And now he's trying to ruin my wedding, but I am not about to let that happen. I told my mother that in no uncertain terms is he invited or allowed to attend, and that if she even considers making a grand entrance, that she will be politely asked to leave, and then escorted out if need be. I reminded her that she only has one daughter, and that this is going to be my only wedding, so that she should choose wisely. I called Valentina and she said that Omar would be happy to step in if need be, but I don't want there to *be* a need, and I'm hoping against hope that she heard me, and that my mother–this crazy person–that somehow she can understand the gravity of the mere suggestion."

I'm finally about to speak when she continues, her words tumbling out, one on top of the other.

"And I'm sorry for shutting you out, but I really did need to take care of this on my own, and I want you to know that I know your heart is in the right place, but you can't always rush in and fix everything. I love you, I know you know that, but Rhonda: you can't be all things to all people. You'll sacrifice too much of yourself. And I need you to understand that I want you there by my side. You're the sister I never had; you're the best friend I could have ever even asked for...but you can't solve this puzzle. Amalia and I have way too much history, and although I'm sure you would have liked to put her in her place, it was my place to do it."

"I get it," I can barely speak as I'm all choked up now, but her words ring true, and my heart has decided to pay attention.

Chapter Forty-Eight

Once we checked in, the only thing that happened...was that Jack forgot his shoes.

Amalia showed up without Pedro, and Dez was happy enough to let it all go for now.

"How did he forget his shoes?" Amalia is one step below outrage, but closing in fast.

"I have no idea Mom, but he did. It's done. There's nothing we can do now," Dez replies through lips that were being perfectly lined by the resort's makeup artist.

"Doesn't anybody else wear the same size shoes?" Amalia rants.

"You know what, Mom? It's fine. I just sent Rhonda downstairs to find the best pair of flip-flops she can find for each of us," Dez points behind her without turning her head, and I hold up the two blingiest pairs of sandals I could find in the resort shop.

(While down there, I poked around to find that the sunblock, although not ninety-two dollars, came in at the bank-breaking price of thirty-seven dollars for ten measly ounces!)

"Why are *you* not going to wear *your* shoes now?" Amalia says, succumbing to full-blown outrage.

"Because WHY SHOULD I?" Dez is yelling now, "We're getting married on the beach. WE SHOULD HAVE WORN FLIP FLOPS TO BEGIN WITH! I NEED TO PEE," Dez extricates herself from the makeup chair for a minute and the room falls silent. Seconds after the bathroom door shuts, Amalia starts speaking to Dez's cousin Valentina in Spanish as Dez shouts from the bathroom, "I CAN HEAR YOU!"

"Look, Amalia, I think Dez is just starting to get a little bit nervous now, so maybe we can..." I trail off as Valentina says something back in Spanish and then Amalia leaves the room.

I look to Valentina.

"I just asked her to please go get me some Advil," Valentina shrugs.

"Good distraction," I nod, then knock quietly on the bathroom door to see how Dez is faring.

"I'm fine." She rips open the door, "Is she gone?"

"Yes, Valentina sent her on an imaginary errand." I pause, "How are you doing?"

"I'm good."

"Breathe."

"I am breathing."

"How about a few deep breaths, in and out?" I demonstrate.

"How about you go bring Jack his sandals?"

"You got it." I do an about-face and leave the room. I pad down the hall to where the guys are getting ready and walk in mid-toast, beer bottles clanked together high in the air.

"To JACK!" they all shout.

"Ah, guys? Hate to interrupt but I'm here to deliver Jack's shoes," I wave the sandals at him.

"Huh," he says as he takes them from me, surveying them quickly. "I think we should go barefoot."

"They were the only ones in your size," I offer.

"No, they're fine. Thank you. I just...let me text Dez," he takes them from me and grabs his phone with the other hand.

"Hey Lady!" My husband comes up alongside me and touches my hair, which is currently hair sprayed within an inch of its life.

"You like?" I went along with whatever the hairdresser thought would be best.

"You look fabulous. Did you remember your shoes?"

"Yes." I lean in and give him a quick kiss. "Now go help your friend...do...whatever," I say.

I leave the room slightly perturbed at the amount of stuff men *don't* have to do to get ready, and I'm just about to expound on this when I reenter Dez's suite.

"Did you bring a pair of flip-flops for yourself?" Dez confronts me at the door.

"A pair? Do you know me at all? I bought three." (Overpacking is my strong suit.)

"I say we all wear the flip flops down the beach and then barefoot it is!" Dez announces as if she just solved the world's problems.

"It's your wedding, and I will do whatever you ask of me." I grab my key card. "I'll be right back."

I run straight to my room and snatch my fanciest pair of

flip-flops off the closet floor, exit the room, think twice, and go back and grab James's pair as well. I make a quick delivery to the boy's room and then double back to Dez.

"Yes!" She nods her head as I walk back in. "I'm thinking I'll have an excuse for Jack to take me dancing when we get back; that way I can wear those." She gestures in the direction of her still boxed pair of electric blue high heels.

"But now you need something blue!" Amalia insists. She's returned from her errand and hasn't said another word until now. Valentina comes to the rescue with a bobby pin she has in her bag, a small blue dragonfly attached. Once Dez's makeup is finished, we start to exit the room as a group. I look to her in the elevator.

"How're you doing?" My eyes search hers.

"I'm good," she insists.

She looks gorgeous. Dez is naturally pretty, but today she looks otherworldly. Her hair and makeup are sheer perfection, and as she stands there tapping her fingers against the elevator wall, I am convinced the dress was made specifically for her.

"You look amazing," I say, already trying hard to not cry and ruin my makeup before the ceremony even begins. By the time the elevator bell dings and we're deposited in the lobby, we all take turns telling her how great she looks.

They chose to get married right before sunset, so there's a cool breeze blowing through the open air lobby and people that are making their way to dinner all stop and stare and wish her luck. Within a matter of minutes, we're joined by the resort's wedding planner Nyla, and she is as excited as a junior bridesmaid.

"You look divine!" She makes a big deal out of fanning herself and then Dez, which cuts the nervousness and makes us all laugh. "Now, are you ready to go get your groom?"

Dez's face lights up and she nods seriously. We follow Nyla out to the main pool area, which is set up like a piazza, with an enormous pool in the middle and little restaurants and shops all around. We cross a bridge and begin to walk towards the beach.

Eventually we end up on a long man-made pier, and I silently thank Jack for forgetting his shoes as the flip-flops are at the very least comfortable for the long trek down the aisle. Nyla asks us to pause a moment and wait, then speaks into some sort of wireless microphone. I hear her assistant's voice come back with barely controlled excitement: "We're ready."

Suddenly, the resort pipes in the music Dez and Jack chose, and we make our way down the aisle, first Valentina, then me, followed by Dez, her arm hooked through Amalia's. My heart is full when I reach the end of the pier and take my place under the gazebo; I see Jack, smiling nervously, Jack's Dad, and my own husband, all looking the epitome of handsome. When I turn, I have to bite my bottom lip to force myself from crying. Dez looks beautiful, and as my heart takes it all in, I feel an over-whelming sense of joy.

The music is turned down, and the vows are traditional. It's simple and it's about them; no fanfare, just two people who love each other framed by a glorious sunset.

I'm pretty sure it's exactly what Dez wanted. It's surreal to me though, when I look back on the countless times Dez insisted she would never get married...and I allow myself to give in to the fact that I'm a witness to a real-life miracle.

Chapter Forty-Nine

A couple of days after the ceremony, everyone was gone except for James and I and the honeymooners. We had opted to stay on a few days for our own vacation, and Dez and Jack planned on returning a couple of days after us.

"Do you know that I can sit here all day, every day, for the rest of my life...and be incredibly happy?" James sighs as he looks out on the Caribbean Sea, the water the shade of blue that you imagine, and crave, and long for, every minute of the endless winter.

"I know this about you," I peer at him from behind my bright red sunglasses and smile. "Nothing you'd miss at home?"

"Nope."

"Wow, that was quick!" I laugh at his swift response.

"I guess I would eventually miss my family, but as much as I love my job..." He takes his sunglasses off now, and gives me a meaningful look. "I know this sounds crazy, but I've missed you." He reaches for my hand.

"I get it." I decide to get up off my lounge chair and make a motion for him to make some room on his. We lucked out this morning, finding two fabulous lounge chairs open, ready, and waiting for us in a private cabana. Dez and Jack had opted for an all-day scuba excursion, so we were finally able to get in some quality couple time. It was just us, a boatload of sunblock, a couple of good books on the table next to us, and two empty champagne glasses from our recently finished drinks. It was paradise, and I wanted to breathe it in forever, just like he did. Once I got myself situated right up against him, I leaned into James and said, "Remember how I told you we have to shuffle through the days in order to get to the moments?"

"Yes," He's so close I can kiss his lips so I reach over to give him a quick kiss, but he lingers. We kiss sweet kisses in the seclusion of our beachside cabana and I taste the sea and salt on his lips.

"Well…" When we finally pull apart, I open my arms wide to the ocean, "This is our moment."

Chapter Fifty

I'm about to bang my head up against the wall, but decide instead to go grab an extra-everything humungous cup of coffee. I've only been back at work for two days, but it feels like I never left.

"Dez back yet?" Helene asks as I tap my foot while waiting for the elevator.

"Tomorrow," I answer with a forced grin. "I can't wait."

It's not the same without her, and now that we're in the thick of the Perfect Protein campaign, I seriously need my sidekick.

Instead I settle for a solo cup of coffee, and just as I'm adding copious amounts of stevia to my brew, I turn around to find Vivian sitting in my favorite chair. I stop for a minute and take her in, surprised that she's right here in front of me. As far as I know, she never comes over to this side of town. A part of me wants to exit quickly and pretend I don't see her, but the part of me that always wants to do the right thing wins this round.

"Is this seat taken?" I gesture towards what is normally Dez's seat.

"Apparently not," she gives me a wry smile. "I thought you worked somewhere over here."

"Yes, this is where Dez and I refuel throughout the day." I smile back at her.

"She's still on her honeymoon?" Vivian asks with feigned interest. She looks uncomfortable, and moreover, tired.

"Yes. I am really not used to going it alone. So what brings you here?" I'm curious.

"I'm waiting for Bunny. She had a follow-up appointment and Ben couldn't take her because he's having a root canal." She rolls her eyes, and I find myself wondering if she's feeling inconvenienced or if the eyeroll is a direct commentary on root canals in general.

"Well," I'm about to try for something neutral, but Vivian interrupts me.

"You know, I've had a whole lot going on recently," she begins, and then launches into a description I couldn't imagine crafting myself about time, and energy, and her calendar. Somewhere in the midst of her very wordy monologue I begin to see a theme: I believe she's trying to apologize for the mix-up with Jill's tea, but I'm not completely sure, and I'm also not sure I can stop her.

I sit and sip my coffee and try and see her from a different vantage point; although she's nobody's victim, she's also an aging woman who seems to have the weight of the world on her shoulders. Does she (still) see me as some strange form of competition? Perhaps. Either way, I decide to finally be the bigger person, and in a split second, I step into the shoes of my mother's daughter.

"You know, Vivian...I know you're busy and all...juggling a

lot of balls…but you know you can always give me a ring if you want to meet me here for a cup of coffee," I hoist my cup in the air as punctuation.

"That would be nice," She nods, her eyes never leaving my face.

It's understood that Vivian has apologized for the earlier snafu and that this is all I'm ever going to get.

I nod my head and push in my chair as I get up to go, unsure about a hug or air kiss. Vivian isn't the huggy type. I make my way back to the office, my coffee almost drained, and right before I enter the building I smile. My mother might have left this Earth way too soon, but she taught me how to deal with everyone and everything. For that I'm grateful.

As I push my way through the revolving door I hear a ding from the depths of my purse.

It's a text notification from Dez, and it says:

We're on our way.

The End

$\mathcal{A}$cknowledgements

For God's gifts and His call can never be withdrawn. (Romans 11:29)

With gratitude to the people who encouraged me to take action, those who cheered me on, and the reader...for letting me tell you a story.

I especially want to thank all the *Merry Hanukkah* readers who asked for more: more Rhonda and James, more Dez and Jack... even Vivian. I truly hope you enjoyed this ongoing story.

Elizabeth Browning was instrumental in planting this very valuable seed: *"Anything is Possible, and Everything is Okay."*

Lindsay Miserandino: As always, you got to the heart of the story. Once again, you're amazing. Thanks for always getting both *it* and *me*.

Uncle Benny: Still the best.

And to our alter egos on the West Coast: we love you and miss you and wish we were at a resort somewhere with you!

To all the *Merry Hanukkah* couples; I am forever blessed to know you. Keep holding it down. Remember God loves you. Period.

Made in United States
Orlando, FL
08 March 2024

44544458R00104